CHASING
PERFECTION

CHASING PERFECTION

Ryan Giggs

with Colin Cameron

Photographs by John Peters

BOXTREE

First published 1998 by Boxtree
an imprint of Macmillan Publishers Ltd
25 Eccleston Place London SW1W 9NF
and Basingstoke

Associated companies throughout the world

ISBN 07522 21698

1 3 5 7 9 8 6 4 2

A CIP catalogue record for this book is available from
the British Library.

Designed by Ryan Baptiste

Printed and bound by New Interlitho

Reprographics by Speedscan Ltd

CHASING PERFECTION

THE
MIND

'IT'S UPSTAIRS, IT'S ALL IN THE HEAD'

I USED TO WAIT UNTIL THE TEAM TALK IN THE DRESSING ROOM
for the motivation I needed to win a game. Or for someone to shout at me before we kicked off. I realise now
that I need to motivate myself.

Alex Ferguson, the manager, always tells me I can't
leave it to anyone else to make the effort to win games.
I've become more aware of this as I've got older. When
players younger than me started getting into the
Manchester United side, I felt more responsibility to be
motivated. And when I captained Wales for the first time,
against Belgium, I realised a lot was up to me, alone.

Playing for Manchester United makes you want to do
well and be a winner. I am always around successful

people, all of whom want to win and be winners. They're always striving to make the difference. I know my team-mates and I know what they're capable of. I see it week in, week out. I want them to respect me, and I have to prove to them that I belong in the side, that I'm worth my place in the team.

My team-mates complain if I make a mistake. But I can't wait until I let them down and cause them to shout at me. It's my responsibility to produce the commitment.

Money doesn't motivate me now. It used to, when I was a teenager. As an apprentice, the win bonuses made a difference. A big difference. Money mattered then. But the more you earn, the less money motivates you, I find. Having more money has the opposite effect to winning more trophies. The more trophies I win, the more I want to win trophies. I'm not like that with the money I've earned. Players today are on good money to win games and to be successful. But that doesn't mean that players try harder when the cash rewards are increased. For me, it is not about the money.

When I see on the television or in the newspaper that Manchester United has made a £15 million profit, or that the club is worth £350 million on the stock exchange, I am interested - it is my club - but it doesn't affect me, personally. I'm a United player. I don't think about the club as being a public limited company. That's the way players are. I want to do well for the team, for the individuals at the club. I'm a footballer. I just want to win games.

Nothing surprises me about Manchester United, the size of it. I'm a local lad. I grew up with the traditions of Manchester United. I've always supported the club and I think of it as the biggest club in the world. It is a big part of the city of Manchester and for those who live there. It dominates the news. I can see how important it is to everyone when I go to charity functions and soccer schools. I can understand it. I can relate to the fans: they know that I supported the club as a boy, in the same way that they do now. I know the places they know. I can appreciate what the club means to the fans by the number who turn up for players' testimonials. It makes me more determined to do well for the club, and for them, the fans.

I've grown up with the history and traditions of Manchester United. I've grown up with the legends of players like Duncan Edwards and George Best. I want to be as good as them. I never saw some of them play but I want to be remembered in the same way that they are remembered. It seems that everyone who saw Duncan Edwards play says he was the best player they ever saw. Sir Bobby Charlton says so. Duncan Edwards must have been awesome.

At the moment I am the present and the future. I don't realise that I am making history. I'm too involved to be aware of it. I think that you only realise you have made history when you stop playing. Then you notice that someone else is playing in your place. Old players always say that your time will come and go. As the young players follow me up through the club I can understand more what the old players meant.

I have the chance to make history. To be remembered in the same way as the great players of Manchester United. This sense of being part of history will be stronger for me when I come to the end of my career, I'm sure. But I want to be remembered as the best: I know that already.

MOST OF MY FAVOURITE FOOTBALLERS FROM WHEN I WAS a young lad were Manchester United players. Even now, I read and hear about the great names from the club's past, and see the extent of what they achieved in the trophy cabinet. I've met some of them. It's inspiring.

As a youngster, I had posters of footballers on my wall, like any other Manchester boy of my age: pictures

of Bryan Robson, Mark Hughes, and of Welsh players like Ian Rush. I ended up playing with some of them. I can understand why young supporters hang posters on their walls. Like me when I was their age, they love football. If I had a different job to playing football, I would probably still have posters on my wall today. The only reason my posters came down was because I started training with my heroes.

I don't have heroes today in the same way that I did when I was much younger. I still respect and look up to all my senior team-mates, but they are not my heroes. With day-to-day contact, Manchester United players could not continue to be my heroes. And it's difficult for

me to have heroes outside football. There are, of course, other sportsmen and sportswomen whose excellence I admire. Michael Jordan, Tiger Woods, Brian Lara - they are all great sportsmen in their own right. But I am not a professional basketball player, a pro golfer or a Test cricketer. For that reason they cannot be an inspiration to me. They interest me, but that's all.

I don't idolise anyone now, but I look to other players, my team-mates and opponents, to see ways in which I can make the best of my opportunities. When I was eighteen and nineteen, an impressionable time, I was lucky to be surrounded in the team by players who were natural winners: Steve Bruce, the captain, Mark Hughes, and later on Paul Ince and Eric Cantona. I used to watch the way Eric trained and rested, how he lived his life. He would give me advice, and I would learn from it. I would be out with Eric and someone would offer him a drink and he would turn it down, because he never drank for four days or so before a game. I took that on board. I don't have role models, but Eric's as close to one as I've had.

I'VE ALWAYS BEEN COMPETITIVE. I'VE ALWAYS WANTED TO WIN. It comes from my parents. My mum played baseball in a league in Wales. My dad was really competitive. When I played football or rugby with him in the park, with my brother, winning always mattered. It was instilled in me then and now extends
into

everything I do. I have played in losing teams and in winning teams. I know which I prefer. I lost my first game of football. We were hammered. I didn't like that. As a schoolboy, I played for Dean's, and Stretford Vics beat us in the cup every year, until finally we beat them. That felt good. Even now, even when I play well, I still find it upsetting if we lose. I'm a bad loser. Always have been.

I'm competitive in all situations. I'm paid to be competitive as a footballer, but I'm still keen to win, whatever the sport or the circumstances, whatever's on the line. Once that competitive edge is inside you, it's always there. There's a part of me that always wants to get better and always wants to win. You can't turn that on and off.

I always knew that I had ability. When I signed for Manchester United some people treated me a bit differently. At school, people knew me and what I had achieved even then. I'd played for England Schoolboys so I was noticed. But it
didn't

happen overnight, and so I didn't become too confident. I don't think I was ever cocky, or that the people I played against when I was younger thought that I was cocky. I just got on with it. In football, I find that it's the Cockneys and Geordies who are the cocky ones, even when they are only fifteen or sixteen. Geordies are brash. Cockneys always have confidence. Not a nasty streak, just a belief that they are good at something. I never take much notice. And I respect my opponents. I don't always do well against the same player. I don't want to motivate them by the way I behave towards them. I don't want to give anyone an added excuse to kick me next time.

In my mind I now know, whoever I am playing, that I can beat them if I am playing well. Anyone. An opponent may be quick, but he may also be a poor tackler. If he's a good tackler, he may be slow. All players have weaknesses and I can exploit whatever those weaknesses happen to be. I have never thought that any player I'm up against has the measure of me. I've never thought, oh no, it's him. Even when I was weaker physically than I am now and many players were stronger than me, it didn't worry me. No player has everything. I always remind myself of that.

When I was younger, if I was suffering a run of poor form, I worried more than I do now about when it would end. When you are a young player, you have to prove yourself. There's a lot of pressure. Experience helps you to cope with that. As I got older, I became better equipped to handle pressure situations and poor runs of personal form. Of course, winning has helped. The medals and trophies have helped.

The manager helps reinforce my self-confidence. Before a game, he will remind me that I had the beating of the full back last time I played against him and that I can do it again, or that the full back can't tackle. It's good to be encouraged, although to some extent it brings some added pressure. I might feel that I have to do well because of it. But I always have confidence in my own ability to cope with the challenge ahead.

I need to be confident. It gives me an extra yard of pace. It makes me sharper all round. I am naturally confident, but I have become more confident with age and experience. It's always nice when someone tells you that you've done well. But with experience I need it less and less. My confidence has grown.

I don't suffer from nerves. Team-mates might talk about the game ahead and say that it's a tough one, but I'm always confident. The few times when I've been nervous I think it might actually have helped my game. There are times when I even wish I was more nervous in the hours leading up to a match because it could help keep me on my toes. It is difficult for me. Most of the teams I've played in throughout my career haven't lost very often.

I do have self-doubts occasionally and I've got to be strong enough to cope with them. I might go through phases when my confidence dips, but it never drops by much. If I have a bad game, I have to remember that I haven't become a bad player overnight. I know that I won't play to the best of my ability every single week, but knowing that makes me more determined than ever to try as hard as I can to keep up the standard through-out the season.

I HAVE GROWN UP MENTALLY WITH THE PRESSURES OF playing for Manchester United and having to perform in front of thousands of supporters. Pressure is negative for some players. For me it's positive. It makes me strive to do better. I'm hard on myself. I have to be tough. Not physically tough. But tough in my head.

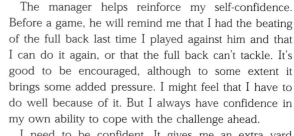

A crowd of two hundred friends, family and school-mates watching an under-12s cup final can be pressure for the young players. Even when you are a bit older, having your parents watch you play football on a Sunday can bring its own type of pressure. I've always wanted to do well for my friends and for my family. When they travel for away games, or when my grand-parents come up from Wales to Manchester for a game, it gives me an extra incentive. I don't have to prove anything to friends and family, but I still want to do well for them. The people who expect the least from me are often the ones I want to impress the most. It's not about proving anything to them. I just don't want to let down people I care about.

With the fans, it is different. I do need to prove myself to them and to keep proving myself. They pay their money and support me, and Manchester United, and Wales, so I want to do well for them. I want to reward their support.

When I was a young player I wanted to impress the older, more established, senior players in the squad. I wanted to prove that I was good enough to be a United player and to play alongside them. Even now, I still want to impress my team-mates. When new players come to the club, I try to prove to them that I'm worthy of a place in the side.

THE PRESSURE OF PLAYING FOR MANCHESTER UNITED COMES from the expectations. We are expected to win all the time. Expectations can create tension and stress. The fear of failure motivates me. In the days leading up to a big game, I feel the tension in the team building up.

There is less joking, everyone seems to train harder. Everything is more focused.

The expectations of me when I play for Wales are more personal. We are not expected to win, like Manchester United, every time we play. But even if Wales lose, people will ask, how did Giggs play? Did he have a good game? There are more match winners in the Manchester United team and people look at the team as a whole. There is more individual pressure on me playing for Wales.

For Wales, I feel that we, as a team, have the beating of our opponents, whoever we are playing. Even when we have played Germany away from home, a match that most people would expect us to lose. For a game like that, I realise that we have a tough challenge, but my confidence is still intact. I know it is going to be difficult, but that doesn't bother me. It was the same when I was playing Sunday League football. I wasn't always in the best team and it might have occasionally been in the back of my mind that we might not win, but I was still prepared to give everything and still believed we could do it. Just because you are not certain to win doesn't mean that you should try any less hard, or accept defeat before the game has even started.

I don't think that, for me, anything will top captaining Wales. I was nervous then. I am not a leader who shouts a lot. I tried to lead by example. I knew we could beat Belgium and I tried to show my team-mates through the way I played that that was what I believed. We went 3-0 down but recovered to 3-2 and we should have drawn 3-3. The players responded. I approach every game believing that we can win. The rest of the team can believe it, too.

I react to personal pressure and responsibility in a positive way. When the Welsh squad is preparing for a game and the coaches tell the players they should try to give the ball to me and let me do what I want with it, it's flattering. I am flattered that they have faith in me, that they think that by giving me the ball during the game the team has a greater chance of winning. A lot of players prefer playing under less pressure, when there are lower expectations. It doesn't bother me. I am proud to play for Wales, where I was born, whatever pressure there is on me as an individual.

IN KEEPING CONFIDENT AND focused, I have to put out of my mind the possibility that I might pick up an injury. It will affect my game if I don't. Fear of injury is a pressure. Injuries are part of the game. Football is played at such a pace today, there are going to be injuries. I think more injuries occur now than when I started playing in the first team.

David Busst broke his leg very badly at Old Trafford playing for Coventry in 1996. Ultimately, it ended his career. The incident affected the whole match. It happened just inside the six-yard box early on in the game. I was on the edge of the penalty area and didn't really see the tackle. I saw Peter Schmeichel waving and calling for the physio and medical team. Then he walked away. I saw the blood. David was lying there screaming in pain and I could see the bone coming out of his shin. All I wanted was for the physios to get to work as soon as possible. Everyone was affected afterwards. The tackling wasn't the same. The crowd, the atmosphere, the whole game changed after that. It was as if everyone was feeling, let's just get the game over with, shall we?

I talked with friends about the tackle, the injury, and what followed the evening after the game. It was the worst injury I'd ever seen. There was a pool of blood in the penalty box. That knocks you back a bit. David was in a Manchester hospital for a long time afterwards. I went to see him with a couple of the apprentices. There wasn't a lot you could say. He'd been in the hospital for seven or eight weeks and they'd carried out about a dozen operations on his leg. The young lads were pretty quiet. It affects people in different ways. I just think that you can't influence things on the pitch. I don't dwell on it.

I have to tackle. In a match, you have to challenge for the ball. You have to take the risk, even if the next game is an FA Cup Final. I can't think about games ahead. Some people suggested that Eric Cantona didn't tackle much after he returned from his suspension, the one he got for kicking out at a fan, but if there was a ball to win he would go for it. It was just that

tackling wasn't Eric's strong point. He had other strengths, and he brought these strengths to the team.

When I challenge, I have to try to protect myself from injury as well as win the ball. I have played against most players often enough now to be aware of who is tackling me, and to make sure, as best I can, that I don't get hurt, without committing a foul myself. I am interested only in the ball. I don't aim to match a defender's aggression. I just want to protect myself. A defender

once came in to tackle me with both feet over the top of the ball and I could see it coming. I knew what he was going to do. But I didn't take account of it - I didn't protect myself - and his studs hit the bottom of my shins. I was angry with myself. I should have looked after myself better. I was lucky not to get hurt.

If I'm coming back from injury, I must not think about suffering a recurrence. When I came back from a hamstring injury that had kept me out for five weeks, I decided I would run at the full back at the first opportunity. I wanted to test my leg to the full and remove any lingering doubt that I might have had that I was not 100 per cent. Before the game I went in early and had a massage. I did some extra stretching, both before and afterwards, but I didn't change my routine other than that. I had to believe in myself that I was fully fit. Some players wear cycling shorts under their match kit to protect their hamstrings. I used to do that. But I don't believe they make a big difference. In this case as in others I think it's upstairs, it's all in the head.

I have learnt to cope with injuries and being out of the side because of them. I used to be really bad. I wanted to play all the time. I was too impatient. Some players get depressed when they are out injured for a long stretch, say five months. I used to get fed up when I was out for five days. I didn't want to be in the treatment room, or even in the gym building up my strength so that I would be fit to return as soon as I'd recovered from the injury. I wanted to play. I'm better about it now. I just want to know what treatment I'm having. I need to know exactly what I can do - walk the dogs, or just relax and let the injury heal - so that I'm back as quickly as possible. I realise the importance of listening to the physios. If I need to have an operation at least I can be confident that everything will be fine afterwards. I've had injuries when I haven't known how long I can expect to be on the sidelines. Mentally, uncertainty is the worst thing about injuries.

When I'm out injured I can't contribute much towards the team's preparation for a game. And that's frustrating. I can't play in a practice match. The manager wants only the players who are available to him so that he can get on with planning. You're with the team before training begins. Then they go out while you go to the treatment room. During training the players chat. There is always banter. It's two and a half hours a day together, but if you are injured you don't see or speak to team-mates. You might see them if they come into the treatment room for something minor or for a massage afterwards, but you're on the fringes of things. You're no longer part of the core. I don't feel a complete outsider. Plenty ask how you are. But I'm not spending time with the team and I miss the dressing room atmosphere, the banter.

If I'm injured, I go to home games, but not to the away games. If an away game is on television I'll watch it. Then I'm no different to everyone else who is watching. I don't listen to the radio. If the match is not on television, I prefer Teletext. Following the game is easier when the team is winning, of course. Watching the team losing is tough. I want to be doing something about it. Either way, I still want to be playing, but it's not so bad to miss a match that we win. Hearing television and radio commentators mention my name during a game and refer to the contribution I might have made only makes me want to get back to full fitness even faster. It is difficult to take that in: hearing commentators saying 'Giggs this and Giggs that' on the television while I'm watching is strange. It's good to hear, at least, that when I'm injured I'm not forgotten.

THE
BODY

I HAVE GOT TO LOOK AFTER MYSELF PHYSICALLY BECAUSE MY livelihood is at stake. It is too important to allow me to neglect myself, my body and my level of fitness. Naturally gifted players, they have the skill and talent and can do things with the ball and make things happen during a match. But all that is of no use if you are not able to perform consistently for ninety minutes, and you'll only be consistent for the whole game if you're in shape.

It means hard work on fitness and there is no avoiding it or getting out of the graft. Eric Cantona had all the natural ability in the world, but he never shirked from training. He came to the club and showed me, and all the young players, how hard he was prepared to work to improve himself, to make himself a better player and to make the most out of his natural ability and talent. Eric brought that attitude to bear when he was with Manchester United.

I've always known how important being fit is. I've always appreciated that keeping my body in shape matters. I've always known what is good for me and what is not and why it is important to work hard on the training ground. I've trained hard all my career because I've always known that it matters.

You get guidance. At Manchester United there are experts to help me and their opinions are always useful. If I don't feel sharp and I want to do more running to get my fitness levels up nearer to the mark then the coaches will have an idea about what might be good for me. But, ultimately, it is up to me. Advice is good, but really it's about what I want. I have to make the effort. I have to put in the work.

The approach to fitness has changed during the years I've spent at Manchester United. It used to be just the

'IF YOU DON'T LOOK AFTER YOURSELF, YOU LET EVERYBODY DOWN'

coach and the manager. Now the club takes care of all its players' needs, and there are specialists available to me in every area of personal fitness and players' well-being. You are working as part of a team and the club is committed to looking after its employees. But it is also about personal responsibility. And I want to play, and make the best of my ability, which means being fit. Being a footballer is my job and I don't want a day off.

WHEN THE SEASON FINISHES, I RELAX FOR SEVEN OR eight weeks. To some extent, I let myself go. I eat more and drink a bit more. I won't be thinking too much about training or doing any serious exercise. Seven or eight weeks off is the sort of break I might suffer if I got injured and after sitting out for that sort of time I only need a couple of weeks to get back in shape. But if I go away on holiday somewhere warm I might swim and stretch a little. Or jog once a week. It is partly because I want to, to feel good, and partly because I don't want to lose all the fitness that I have built up over the previous season. It's a bit of both these things. Wherever I am, it's always in the back of my mind that it might be worthwhile having a run on the beach every seven days or so. Or having a swim to keep myself supple.

As a first-year and second-year apprentice at Manchester United, when I was a teenager, I used to run a lot in the week before preseason fitness training began. I wanted to be ready, to have a head start. I don't do running in the week before preseason training now because modern football fitness training is not about running for miles and miles to build up stamina. That's part of it, and I know that bit is always going to be hard, but during preseason training the distances I cover running become shorter and shorter.

Preseason training at the Cliff, Manchester United's training ground, used to be about running ten miles of cross-country. Now it is more controlled. There is some stamina work, some long-distance running, but I really build up fitness over a fortnight more by working with the ball. There is a warm-up lap to start with, round the pitch, and one to finish, but Brian Kidd, the assistant manager, who with his experience almost qualifies as a fitness instructor in his own right, will calculate roughly how much running we've done in a day as part of the general training and decide how much more we need to do during any single session the next day and throughout preseason training fortnight.

Brian Kidd travels all over Europe, to Italy and Juventus, to Holland and Ajax, to see how they train and condition themselves. He has learnt the continental techniques used abroad to get players fit and to keep them fit and he applies what he has learnt to our own regime. During the season, he varies the amount of training we do depending on what games are ahead and what we've played. If there's been no midweek game we may work on stamina before a weekend match.

There can be a huge amount of repetition in all training. The coaches do their best to keep it varied and challenging, to make it different so that it doesn't feel like the same old routine. There are five-a-side matches, and shooting, training that players can enjoy and that doesn't feel monotonous. Brian Kidd is always asking me and my team-mates what we think of the training, whether we enjoyed it. He has been a player for Manchester United and at other clubs so he knows that training can become boring if there is no variety and no challenge to it. It needs an edge and to be fresh.

Training is competitive. When a new player comes to the club, he wants to impress. In five-a-side games, the younger players group together to take on the more experienced ones, which adds an edge. Few players plod through training. Alex Ferguson and Brian Kidd would not let them. The older players have to be just as dedicated. The edge is always there. There are times when practice matches have to stop because the tackles are flying in. The team spirit has always been there during my career, but the competitive edge means that I have seen players have to be separated when things get too heated.

Preseason training, generally, is less important to the younger players. Older players - and I still consider myself young - benefit from preseason training more and need it more as they get older. As you age you become physically more solid in the waist and chest and in the legs. With this you can lose speed and sharpness over the summer and you will need preseason training to bring it back. It won't always return. I'm a speed and touch player. Those are my strengths. But I don't worry that as my career develops I may lose some of my speed. There's no point in worrying about it until it actually happens. If it does, I'll adapt my game. Like John Barnes. In his early days, he was quick, and sharp. He could beat players just through his speed. As he got older he relied more on passing the ball to take out defenders and with experience of matches he became a different sort of player, but no less effective. He developed his game to compensate for the loss of speed he suffered. He may even have become a better player as he grew older. If it happens to me, if I lose some of my speed, I'll adapt, too. I might become a slower player, but I don't have to become less effective with it. Nobody does.

For now, at least, speed is my greatest strength. When we've had to complete some laps of the pitch or sprints, I'm usually first in training. I always want to be first. When I used to train with Paul Ince, before his transfer to Italy, he'd warn me against finishing first in the runs. He said the coach and manager would expect me to finish first every year, and when faster players joined the club or came up through the ranks and I finished only third or fourth, they would think that I wasn't fit. I'll never be the sort of player who feels fine about coasting in third or fourth. I always have to be first. Some players are never first. That doesn't mean they're not fit, or that the manager suspects they might be slacking. Some also struggle in preseason, but have the stamina and sharpness when it matters. Roy Keane is not the best before the season starts yet he can run all day in games.

I would not benefit much from spending too long in the gym lifting heavy weights. Sprinters lift heavy

weights to give them power but their power - the ability to run flat out for only 100 metres - is not the mix of power, speed and strength I need for football. In building up my body strength I am better off lifting lighter weights, quickly. Or boxing with a coach who wears pads on his hands for me to hit. Or skipping, which strengthens my body and develops speed of movement and not just power.

I'VE ALWAYS BEEN HEALTHY. I DIDN'T SUFFER ANY OF THE common children's ailments. Some players have asthma which affects them during preseason training and friendlies abroad when the air is heavy. I have never smoked. Some players do when they are out socialising or enjoying a drink after a game, but I've never been tempted. People don't always believe this, that I've never tried even a single puff, but it just doesn't appeal to me. My mother has never smoked and my dad didn't, not until he was older. At school, there was a group of us who went around together and two or three tried it, but even then I didn't see the point. To be honest, I think it is a disgusting habit.

Obviously, I have been ill and had my share of health problems. I had my tonsils out at the end of the 1995 season. The idea was to take out my wisdom teeth at the same time. After the operation I was told to stay in bed for ten days, but I decided to walk the dogs after only three nights. I felt fine getting up, but as soon as I walked out the door I began to feel dizzy. I suddenly felt very tired. The doctors weren't joking when they said ten days.

Keeping healthy through the season can be difficult. At Manchester United, there are sixty or seventy professional footballers all sharing facilities, men in the same building every day breathing the same air. It means that viruses and flu can spread very quickly. Athletes are also stretching their bodies to the limit physically and that can make them more vulnerable to a virus that may mean a day off from the job.

I don't avoid my friends outside the club if they have a cold or flu any more than anyone else might avoid friends away from work. I can't live in a bubble or wrapped in cotton wool. But, at the club, if you go down with something, wherever it has come from, then it's straight home, especially if it's flu. The club doesn't want flu to spread so anything that can be done to limit the risk of that happening will be done, starting with isolating the unlucky ones until they are in the clear.

The club can only react to illness like the flu or different types of virus. Players are all individuals and it isn't possible to monitor everyone. I monitor my own health. If I am feeling tired, I will ask the club dietitian whether I am eating the right things and what I should eat to give me more energy. If it's more serious than that, if I'm not sleeping, or if I'm feeling seriously under the weather, then I'll see the doctor. It's just another personal responsibility.

There will always be days when you don't feel 100 per cent right. It's normal for me - or any professional

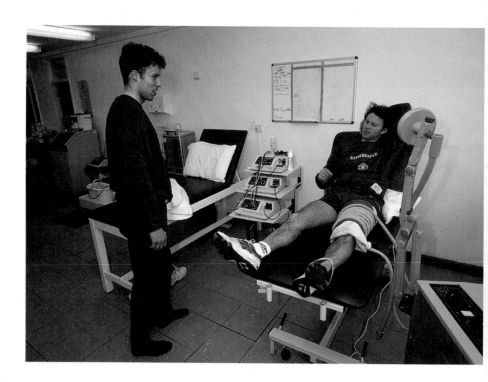

footballer - to have some days that are better than others, physically speaking, and some days that are worse. There are great days, when I might have slept badly but I will come into training and be absolutely flying. But, maybe once a week, when I have had a good ten hours' sleep and should feel great, I'm just tired. It can be because of a game I've played two or three days before, which has finally caught up with me, or because we did some extra running in training the day before. Everyone has good days and bad days. Whatever you do.

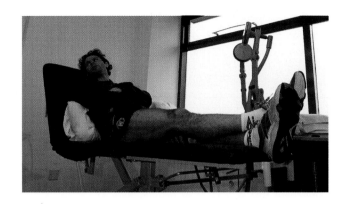

The dietitian can help in countering bad days and tiredness. Diet has changed so much, even during my time at Manchester United. When I was fourteen or fifteen and coming to the club during the summer holidays, the club canteen had everything: chips, eggs, sausages - a normal choice, the same as in any canteen at work. There was chocolate sponge cake, which was always my favourite. Today, however, the choice is much healthier.

I am not particularly curious about food and what I eat. I tend to eat healthy food without even thinking about it. I've never had to worry about my weight. The important figure is not so much my absolute body weight as my body-fat ratio. The club doesn't want it to be much more than 15 per cent. Mine has never been higher than 8 per cent. It has never been a concern. I'm training practically every day during the season, so I'm not going to put weight on. It wouldn't really matter that much if I occasionally ate fatty food during the season.

The only thing that is really important is that I make sure I eat plenty of carbohydrates in the two days before a game. That means plenty of bread, vegetables and foods like pasta. I have got to make sure I've taken on enough fuel. It is up to me. Only I know exactly what I'm eating and it's my responsibility to do the right thing. I don't have a problem with that. You can train as hard as you like, but if you eat the wrong food, you won't perform. If I don't eat enough carbohydrates and take on the energy I need, then I know I won't perform in a

game. I'm eating for that purpose, and not for pleasure.

The same applies to drink. Liquids are as important as food. You can't perform if you are dehydrated. I must take on enough water before training and afterwards, and on match days as well as at half-time during a game. Coffee, tea and alcohol can all dehydrate you so I watch my intake of these close to a game. It's no sacrifice. If I don't, I won't reproduce my best form. And if I don't reproduce my best form, what's the point in putting in all the hard work at the training ground? You've got to watch what you eat and drink so that all the effort before a game is not wasted.

The other essential during the season is that I get plenty of rest when I am not playing or training. I try to sleep from around 11.30 p.m. until nine in the morning. If I wake up in the middle of the night, or have trouble getting to sleep after a game that kicked off in the evening, it is frustrating, but I have to try to get to sleep. Rest is so important. If you don't look after the amount of rest, you can become tired and run down and that is letting yourself down. And if you don't look after yourself, you let everybody down. It's as simple as that. And, of course, you lose your place in the side. There's a big incentive to take good care of yourself.

I have never broken a bone. I have never really even feared that I might have broken something playing. I've had plenty of X-rays. The club is very cautious and if you pick up a knock or fall badly or heavily then you'll be sent straight away for a check to see if anything has been broken. Apart from one occasion, when I shot and in following through hit the studs on the bottom of an opponent's boot with the top of my own foot, I haven't really ever thought after a tackle that I might have cracked a bone.

I felt that injury for seven or eight months. It was a part of my foot which is unprotected. Whenever I kicked a ball after that I felt some pain. I'd damaged the ligaments on the top of my foot and it hurt for a long time.

I've had a hernia operation. People think a hernia is something that affects older people, but it is quite a common injury with young players. I thought the operation was going to be pretty painful. I had seen players with sixteen staples in their stomachs where the surgeon had operated and the scar always looks sore. It was, to a certain extent, but for me it ended up not being as bad as it looked. The surgeon who operated on me talked me through the procedure beforehand, which put my mind at rest. Since then, I have talked to others - but without mentioning the scars or staples - who are also facing the operation, and have tried to reassure them that it's not as bad as it seems.

Before the hernia operation cleared up the problem, I was in great pain whenever I tried to run. I couldn't sprint, or lift off from a standing start. When I stood on my right leg there was a dull pain like toothache and when I tried to do any more the pain would become stabbing. I had no power. As the months went on I was able to do less and less, until finally I couldn't do anything at all.

It was a while before I was diagnosed as having a hernia problem. In some ways, it was a relief when a hernia was finally confirmed. I was disappointed. I knew it meant I'd miss games, but at least I knew what was wrong with me and that after the operation I had every chance of being absolutely fine in five to seven weeks. Long-term injuries for players - when they keep trying to get back to full fitness and then break down after a hard session or a comeback match - are frustrating. You think you're going to be back playing again in four weeks, and then you are told that it will be longer. I always have to

try to remember that most players do make a complete recovery. There's a lot of bad luck in football, but you must be patient and listen to the fitness coaches, doctors and surgeons.

IF I PICK UP AN INJURY IN A MATCH AND I AM SUBSTITUTED then I go immediately to the treatment room. It can mean a much quicker recovery. If it is a muscle tear or strain then there can be internal bleeding and ice will stem the flow and speed up the healing process. Other injuries don't emerge until the next day, long after the match is over. There can be some discomfort during the game, but adrenaline masks pain and the full extent of the knock. It may only start to hurt badly when you wake up the next day.

When Manchester United play in Europe, the physios travel with the team so they're on hand to treat any injuries. The equipment in the medical room at the training ground is state-of-the-art and can be transported easily. Players recovering from long-term injuries can even travel with the team and continue their rehabilitation programme away from the Cliff. Roy Keane and Terry Cooke were both recovering from knee ligament injuries. They'd been out for five months, and when the team went to France they went along. They worked on the exercise bikes while the team prepared for the quarter final of the Champions' Cup against Monaco. I was out with a hamstring injury. The physios decided that sitting on a plane would not be good for it at all. So I stayed at home, but the trip helped stop Roy and Terry from becoming mentally stale or depressed. Travel and a different environment relieves the boredom of recuperation.

When I'm injured, I have to trust the physios and everyone else who is trying to restore me to fitness. I once had a trapped nerve in my hand. The physio went straight away to massage the back of my shoulder and that immediately made the hand feel better. My thumb was sore so I'd assumed the solution was in treating the thumb. As usual, the physio knew better. I had damaged a nerve that stretched back up the arm to my shoulder, and it was there that the pain could be alleviated.

You have to let the physios get on with their work. You must also tell them exactly what you are feeling. They are experts and know exactly what treatment is needed. But they won't be able to help unless you explain exactly where the pain is and how it feels, every day, day after day, until you are fully fit and back playing. The physios supervise stretching and ask how it feels so they can decide how far you can go in training. When you are back running, to get the circulation going to help the healing, the physio jogs alongside you to talk

to you and gauge what you are feeling. The physio reassures you as you feel your way back to full fitness.

WHEN YOU PULL A HAMSTRING IT FEELS LIKE YOU'VE BEEN stabbed in the back of the leg with a knife. In February of the 1998 season I pulled a hamstring badly against Derby County. As soon as I started to run I felt it go. The sharp pain told me that I had to stop immediately. I knew straight away that I had a serious problem.

I had to leave the injury completely alone for about a week so that the leg muscle could settle down. There was a hole and it moved around the back of the leg. At first it was at the top of the leg and it then moved down to the bottom. Ice on the day had helped stop the internal bleeding and after a week I was able to start moving again: walking, stretching, jogging. The ice was crucial in enabling me to start exercising again within seven days of the injury.

After I began very gentle exercise, the injury began to get better, but not at an even pace. It would improve a lot overnight and then seem to stall. Progress would be good but then there would be setbacks. I'd go to sleep and the next day the hamstring might feel better, but sometimes it was worse. This was hard to cope with mentally. I had expected to be out for six weeks. Then I'd begin to think that it might not be so long after all, only to be disappointed.

Regaining the last 10 per cent of full fitness was the toughest part. Early on in the rehabilitation, I went quite quickly from the medical room to riding the exercise bike, doing weights in the gym and then jogging and running. But the return to full fitness dragged on. It was frustrating. The results for Manchester United while I was out weren't good, which made it even harder.

ACHIEVING FULL MATCH FITNESS ONLY COMES WITH GAMES. There is a sharpness I need. If I haven't been playing games, I will have lost my edge. When I eventually come back from an injury like a hamstring pull I might feel better at the end of a comeback game than at the beginning. That's because I might have felt fresher mentally, because I haven't been playing and the pressure's been off. And as I'm naturally fit, having already played games in the season I retain my stamina even during a four- or five-week lay-off. But I lose the half a yard in five at the beginning of a run which will only return with playing games.

Whatever training you do, it cannot substitute for the demands that are made on you during a game. Nothing you can do in training compares to the demands of ninety minutes of football. Brian Kidd cannot recreate the conditions of a game on the training ground. I have actually to play to become sharp again. Some sharpness will come from training and some added stamina will come from jogging round the pitch and sprinting across it, but during a game there's also stopping, changing direction, tackling, getting up, jumping for headers. Sliding tackles take a lot out of me. We train for them using tackle bags. But I cannot acquire all the fitness and sharpness I need to tackle just from training. I can only do that by playing.

Some players can cope with injuries and still play. I've known players play with a strained hamstring all the time. Steve Bruce was one. Paul Ince could hide his injuries. Players like them end up in the treatment room the day after the game, but somehow they always seem to be able to nurse themselves through, game after game, until the end of the season when they at last allow themselves to rest. It depends, to some extent, on where you play. If you're a striker, you'll have to sprint throughout the game, and the demands made on your body will be different to those made on a defender. But it's really down to the individual. It's down to how you feel in yourself.

I need to be 100 per cent right. I am a speed player and as speed is my main asset I can't get away with a slightly strained hamstring. During the 1994/5 season, I played on with a bad hamstring - the other leg to the one I pulled against Derby - and the injury dragged on for weeks. If you're not 100 per cent fit and you think you might not make your usual contribution then you

shouldn't say you're fit to play. You'll let your team-mates down if you do.

I don't talk that openly about injuries. If I'm asked when I expect to be back playing, I usually repeat what I've been told by the physios, rather than whatever I'm hoping for. Sometimes I don't know exactly what's wrong with me. If that's the case, I certainly can't say when I expect to be back - it could be six weeks, a month, whatever.

We're not encouraged to talk about injuries. If there is a doubt about when a player is due to play again, or whether myself or a team-mate is going to be fit for a big match, then the uncertainty can be turned into an advantage. The team knows. We see each other at the training ground and talk among ourselves about injuries. But the opposition only find out who's playing on match days, just before kick-off. Keeping information about who's fit and who's injured within the club can provide an edge. The medical room is off-limits to anyone outside the players and team management, and this can pay off on the pitch.

If fans and followers of the game knew more about the ins and outs of footballers' fitness, and what players go through during a season, they might be more sympathetic when someone is having a bad game. Players play with injuries and some have injections to take the pain away so they can get through a game. In every season there will be times when things don't work out. It just happens - to me, to everyone. If I'm having a bad game, it is never because I'm not trying.

PREPARATION

As a team, we take a long hard look at our opponents and the way they play before every game. We are looking for their weak points and the ways we can capitalise on them and exploit them. We study our opponents' best players and see how best to stop them being effective. We are looking for ways to contain the opposition.

Alex Ferguson and Brian Kidd discuss the opposition. Before we have a practice match in which some players will try to play in the style we expect to face in our next match, there are questions. Any thoughts of your own can then be raised.

People can make a big deal about bogey teams, teams they think have done well against me and Manchester United in the past. When we are due to play teams who can claim some success over us there are some comments before the game and some players like to talk about it. I think it can put some doubt in your mind about the game ahead. It can also make you want to do better, which is a positive reaction to a negative thought, but I don't think about it for long, either way. I don't let it bother me. In truth, there are not many teams who can claim to have done consistently well against Manchester United during the time I have been playing. There are always positives to look at, even from games where we have lost. Southampton have done well against us at the Dell. They beat us 6-3 one year. But in that game we scored three times away from home. If you worry too much about the negatives that have occurred in past encounters you can try too hard, instead of trying to play your normal game which has brought success in the past. There are always some positives to focus on in defeat. When you hit the post, when you forced the keeper into making a good save.

You can plan too much. You can overelaborate and prepare in too much detail for situations like corners and free kicks. Some teams - like Wimbledon - spend time on corner routines. I've never played in teams who have dwelt too long on set pieces and corners. These are a chance to attack the right areas around the goal from which the opposition can be punished. Our opponents may be strong defensively and it may mean that I have to vary my delivery, but the quality of the delivery on the day, in the match, is more important than whether a complex free-kick routine works.

The players I play with are capable of hitting the target with a free kick from up to 35 yards, or picking out someone unmarked in the box. If the player has the talent to react to the circumstances, then let him use it to exploit the situation. Let the player express himself. There's no point overcomplicating things when you have the sort of natural talent in a team that we have at Manchester United. From a free kick all you want to do is increase the chances of scoring, and you best achieve that by concentrating on delivering a quality ball and allowing your team-mates to improvise. At United we have a certain way of playing. Individually, we all have jobs to do for the benefit of the team, but I am also free to express myself - from free kicks and in open play.

I have never gone into a game not wanting to win in ninety minutes, and I don't think many other teams do. Some teams, especially in the World Cup and in European football, play for extra time and a penalty shoot-out. I know very quickly if the team we are playing is looking to take it all the way to a shoot-out. I am man-marked and the opposition doesn't look to press the midfield and chase possession. It is frustrating, especially when you know you are the better team. Two teams should always be looking to win in normal time, without the match going into extra time or ending up in a penalty shoot-out. That is how the game should be played.

Extra time doesn't really come into my mind until at least seventy-five minutes of normal time have passed. Then, if the scores are level, it might occur to me that there is an extra half hour to score, on top of what time remains. Thinking about it before then doesn't make sense. It's not good use of the time before a game to spend it discussing the possibility of an extra thirty minutes' football. How often is there extra time? Not often enough for the possibility to be worth considering and preparing for even before kick-off.

'THERE IS NO ROOM FOR NEGATIVE THOUGHT'

With penalty shoot-outs, which follow extra time, practising taking penalties before the game will obviously make you more likely to score, but what's more important is being confident that you're going to score. It doesn't matter whether you're a centre forward, or a centre half, if you believe you're going to score you usually will, and you should try to be one of the first to take a penalty in any shoot-out. Blast it, place it, whatever you feel most confident doing. But expect to score. I missed a penalty in an FA Cup shoot-out at Old Trafford - I blasted it - and I don't think I was really confident about scoring at any stage of the penalty.

It would depress me if a manager said to me, we are playing for penalties. It would mean that we were planning to play a frustrating, negative game, and it's never good if the team feels restricted. I can understand why teams sometimes do. In the FA Cup, a lower league or non-league team has to consider what's the best way to get through to the next round. For them negative tactics might be it. But I can't imagine that the players enjoy it, or that anyone enjoys watching it. There's also the chance that your opponents might be confident about winning on penalties anyway. I can't see it ever happening at Manchester United.

As part of my individual preparation for a match, I might have a reserve team run-out. I've never played regularly for the reserves as I leapfrogged from the youth team into the first team, but I have occasionally turned out as part of an effort to reach full match fitness. If I'm being honest, on the few occasions when I have played it has usually been more for myself and less for the rest of the reserve team. I want to win - I always do - and do well, but, if I have been injured, the match for me is mainly

about checking on my own fitness. This can make full motivation difficult to achieve. In truth, I probably want more than anything just to get through the ninety minutes without a recurrence of whatever has been keeping me out of the first team. It might be a cold, wet Tuesday night. The game might even have been specially arranged for me. It is only natural that I might struggle to be as motivated about winning, especially after having played regularly for the first team in front of over 50,000 at Old Trafford.

The reserves are made up of first-team players who might be struggling for fitness or form, and youth team players making their way up to the first team. It is often a different starting line-up from week to week, made up of players with different objectives. There isn't the rhythm you have between players who play together on a regular basis. I have to rely on professional pride taking a hold in a reserve game. My strong competitive nature will always have an effect, whatever the status of the match. If we go a goal down, suddenly I will want to win the game badly. My team-mates are the same. I know the reserves from the training ground so there's team spirit. And getting kicked doesn't hurt any less.

Spending time before a game fine-tuning skills is rare. There isn't very much time to think about skill and technique once the season has started. I might play on Wednesday, have to have treatment for an injury on Thursday, then have only a short training session on Friday before a game on Saturday and I have to rest for the match. That leaves little time for improving skills and technique. It's a pity. You have to spend time building up confidence on the training ground. Clubs today have their centres of excellence - I attended Manchester City's as a youngster before switching to United - where

players learn all the basics in ball control, often using small-sized footballs, which is very good practice. After an hour of learning, it's just a case of practice and repetition to perfect control, tricks, skills and dribbling so you can reproduce them during a match. That doesn't change with age. It's all about spending the time.

If there is time, I stay behind after a morning's training to practise. I may not be trying something new. Just an effort to improve myself and what I can already do reasonably well. I might try free kicks with my weaker right foot, or practise controlling the ball and passing wearing one boot so that I don't use my stronger left leg. I watch other players practising and try to learn from them, to see how they do things. When Lee Sharpe was at Manchester United I would ask him how he crossed the ball so well. I ask David Beckham how he strikes free kicks.

You can always improve your old skills. Improving what you are already good at is important. Simple things. Taking a penalty and placing it, perfecting that, and then adding more power, or trying to place the ball in a different corner. Dribbling between cones is straight forward, but it can make you quicker with the ball at your feet. Standing at the sideline and crossing balls for fifteen minutes can improve delivery. It's important to remember the basic things. Simple drills help. Any sport coach will recommend that players go back to basics.

If I see a player try something on television, I'll try in training myself to see if I can copy it. I'll see Roberto Carlos on television and think, I'll try that on the training ground. I'll try to reproduce the movement straight away. I break it down into its moving parts and then try to follow them all through in sequence as a whole before trying it at speed and on the move.

Coming back from an injury, I need to restore the touch part of my skills. After a break my crossing might be out and crossing in practice matches helps me regain my accuracy. Like setting a rifle sight after a gun hasn't been used for six months. The basic training means that I feel the ball at my feet again. I need that.

FOR AWAY GAMES, THE ROUTINE MAKES IT A BIT LIKE BEING IN the army. All the travel, the hotels: it can be boring. People think that staying in a hotel must be luxury, but it's not home. I prefer being surrounded by my own possessions at my own place. The aim, for league games which require an overnight stay, is usually to arrive around half an hour before dinner. I unpack and then eat a meal which might have been prepared by our own chef (they sometimes travel with us). After dinner, some players sit and chat and others play snooker or cards. I usually sit in my room and maybe watch television. It's eat, sleep, play, get the job done and then return home where I always feel more comfortable.

The players spend so much time together. Because of this, there is no real need to build up team morale: it comes naturally enough. When we are in a hotel for an away game we split up into our pairings to share rooms but we're together for meals. The dinner table serves to bring us all together. We also travel as a team. As we spend so much time together anyway, there is no need for the manager to arrange for nights out or group entertainments. We all get on without it. Players, and their wives and partners, all socialise together away from the match anyway. It is only natural, and team spirit grows in this way without anything artificial to help it. You can't fake team spirit. It has to be real for it to last.

The Manchester United team is quite unusual. By and large, we have grown up together and that helps create team spirit. But groups will always form, even in a team as closely knit as United. You will always like some team-mates more than others. The older players might stick together. This is also only natural. The manager has to think about this when he plans to bring in players from outside: youngsters, or transfer signings. It is a delicate balance.

When I play for Wales, the captain takes on a lot of the responsibility for building up the squad's spirits during the time the players are together. As international team-mates we see much less of each other so team building can be important. If the captain says that the

players are going out for a drink, then everyone goes out for a drink. It's relaxed, but it's important that everyone joins in, because team spirit can make up for any shortcomings in technique on the field. Rapport matters to the Wales team and it can help us get results against countries who are stronger than we are.

I don't think the captain has that big an influence on the pitch during games. Natural leaders usually emerge in a team by the way they play. They may not even be the captain. It's not like in cricket where a captain makes all the key decisions. A great goal or a big tackle can raise the spirit of the team, just as much as the captain shouting encouragement can.

When I was captain for Wales for the first time, I only knew for sure the day before the game. In the build-up to the match, the more experienced players helped me by taking responsibility for a lot of things off the pitch and by organising distractions for the team to keep everyone fresh and relaxed for the game ahead. That says a lot about the spirit in the Welsh squad. Even when I've missed some friendlies, I always know that I'll be part of the set-up and banter when I play for Wales. I know some of the players from the days when I played for the under-21s and I spend five or six days at a stretch with the senior players, sometimes travelling with the squad to matches abroad.

I'VE BEEN TO MOST COUNTRIES IN EUROPE, WITH EITHER United or Wales. What do I think about the places I have visited? I've seen virtually nothing of them. Budapest and Prague are beautiful cities, but I don't have the chance to enjoy that. I see the airport, the hotel, the stadium. You are detached from the locals for the trip. I am also isolated by not speaking the local language. We arrive, check in to the hotel and have a training session at the stadium the night before the game. Then it's home.

Travelling doesn't prevent me keeping my thoughts on the game. I'm still with my team-mates. The waiting - in airports, on the coach - can be hard, in the same way that lying around in a hotel room in the afternoon before an evening kick-off is boring. But when the game starts, it doesn't matter how far I might have travelled. Or where I am. That never crosses my mind. I have already put the journey behind me.

Coach journeys can be boring. I have got used to them. I try to switch off. Whatever I do - chat with team-mates, listen to music, read a magazine - I try to switch off. I must try to relax.

I dislike flying. My mum has never liked it and I must have got it from her. Of course, I fly if I have to. And we travel to quite a lot of games by plane these days. I flew to Southampton in a small plane for the league fixture there, but I didn't enjoy it. and I generally don't, especially the taking off. I prefer the train.

Relaxing on a plane to a European game is hard. Journalists usually share the flight with us and the atmosphere is different, less natural, than a flight when the team is alone. During the journey there's pressure to do interviews. Normally I'm too busy. There isn't the time to answer questions about the game ahead. But on a flight to Europe, there's plenty of waiting around in airport lounges. Journalists and the public are in contact with you for most of the day. It all adds to the general stress of travelling and, for me, of flying.

After the match it is sometimes straight to the airport. Just two days of eat, sleep, train and play and then it's back to the airport and home. You might go outside the hotel for a bit but for no more than a short walk. That's why I've seen so little of the cities I've played in.

This is the routine for a professional footballer. I've done it since I was a schoolboy. Preseason tours are better. With the whole season ahead of you, the pressure is less and you have more free time to enjoy local sights and traditions. I'd like to experience the great cities of Europe I've already visited, Volgograd, Budapest, Prague, but for now I accept the limits on my freedom to enjoy them because I know that when I travel to these places I'm not on holiday. It's work and I'm there to do a job. I am employed by Manchester United and I don't want any distractions that might affect my performance. I must be ready for the build-up to the game on match day, and the match itself.

I EAT FOR THE LAST TIME THREE HOURS BEFORE THE GAME. MOST players have a set programme for what they eat for their prematch meal, and for the day before. I try to keep my own diet flexible. I doubt there's much difference between having chicken and having steak twenty-four hours before the game. And if you always have to have the same food before a game, then the one occasion when for whatever reason it is unavailable to you - maybe when you are playing abroad - it can create doubt in your mind. Have I had enough of the right food? This is more mental than physical. If I've eaten plenty of carbohydrates and fruit, and taken on plenty of water, I know that I'm ready, prepared. It all helps in remaining confident.

Whether it's morning, afternoon or evening, I'll adjust as much as possible so that I'm physically ready. My body clock has to adjust as best it can.

Mentally, I try to keep my mind free of outside thoughts, whatever the kick-off time. I don't want it clogged up with anything that might distract me. I prefer morning kick-offs. Then it's not a long day spent waiting for the game. I wake up and go pretty much straight into the prematch routine without thinking. Immediately I'm clued up for the match. I find 3 p.m. a sort of nothing time. Evening kick-offs are better than afternoons. Then I have a sleep in the afternoon and when I wake up the match is right upon me.

Whatever the kick-off time, I prepare in the usual way. If I had a good game last time I played I try to stick to the same routine, but I'm not obsessive about it. I don't have complicated rituals that I must follow on match days. Footballers are generally superstitious, but that isn't because they are mentally weak. It is just an individual's way of preparing himself. Gary Neville used to have a music tape that we would play on the coach on the way to games. It would never have bothered me if I hadn't heard it before a game. But there was no harm in playing it again if we had won the week before. I just want the time to pass smoothly. I don't want anything to get in the way of my own preparation.

As kick-off gets closer and closer, there's no room for negative thoughts about the game, or for anyone who doubts their own or the team's ability to do the job in hand. There's joking and plenty of banter, but if the prospect of the match is making you nervous you don't say. Otherwise everyone will find out and then the jokes start flying. It's the way of the team. Teasing and mickey-taking are part of how the dressing room works. It never goes too far and it keeps the spirits up. Every team needs players who break the tension during a season and in the build-up to a big game. Dean Saunders does it for Wales. He is one of the funniest men I have ever known.

About an hour and a half before kick-off, the manager will deliver his final instructions. The emphasis is on tactics, what we can expect from our opponents, what we have to do ourselves. Sometimes the team talk lasts for fifteen minutes, sometimes thirty-five, sometimes just five minutes. The content is the details of the game: what we might be about to face and what problems we might encounter. Sometimes team talks can be quite funny. Two are rarely the same. The atmosphere is relaxed with maybe a bit more of an edge if it's a big game. There's always a danger that the mood can be too relaxed. If the manager feels that, he will counter it. The mood can switch very quickly if he wants it to.

The team talk for Wales focuses much more on organisation. For many games, Wales start as underdogs and the need to be organised against sides who are considered to be technically better footballers is important. It is new opposition every time, and different players filling different roles. We don't play that often together so the build-up is about making sure everyone knows their job in the team, at set pieces, defending and attacking, in open play.

During Alex Ferguson's team talk you just listen. At the end, the manager may direct a particular point at me and then, if I disagree, I can make my own point. You need to be able to say what you think without anyone taking a grudge with them out on to the pitch.

There is some talk about the referee. I know all the Premier League referees now. I have my views about who is good, but I don't dwell on who is refereeing. As a team, there is nothing we can do about it. Whoever is

refereeing, we have to accept it and get on with the game we're playing.

After the general talk, the manager tries to motivate us individually. He might tell me that I'm about to have a great game. Most players need that last bit of encouragement. He'll put something in your mind, something that has happened recently and you'll take the thought with you out on to the pitch. It usually helps. But it's extra to the self-motivation I know I need.

For really big games the atmosphere is quite hyped up; for others there's less anticipation. I try to keep my concentration at the same high level for every game but it's human nature that you are more keyed up for some games than for others. It happens.

My physical warm-up before the game is my own personal routine. Most grounds have a special warm-up room, about the same size as the dressing room, with space for stretching. This keeps me moving and my mind busy and focused. If I'm substitute I usually know the day before. I stretch in the normal way and hope to get on the pitch at some point - partly to prove the manager wrong if I've been dropped - but I have to put my own thoughts to one side and try to encourage the players who are starting the match. Obviously, when I'm not starting from kick-off, I'm less involved, but I don't want the team to do less well just so that I can get on. That doesn't come into it.

I try to stay relaxed, right up to about twenty minutes before kick-off. You can laugh and joke on the pitch when you're going through the final warm-up before returning to the dressing room for the last few minutes ahead of kick-off. Different players have their own way of doing things, but I like to sit and chat with my teammates about anything, the game, whatever comes into the conversation. I don't need to isolate myself from everyone, like some sprinters do before they run the 100 metres. I don't need to achieve mental 'tunnel vision'. Football is not the same discipline as athletics. It's a team game. I've not played with many people who don't want to talk before kick-off.

I don't really think that hard about the game itself and what I am about to do until there are only those twenty

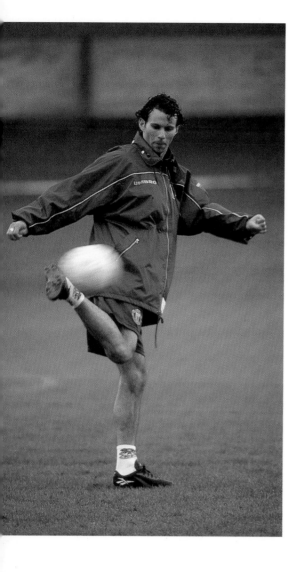

minutes to go. I want to keep my mind uncluttered and fresh. Some players look for friends and family in the crowd before kick-off. I don't. I am concentrating. They understand. I have to be focused.

When the kick-off is close, the mood in the dressing room changes. Suddenly it's serious. The manager senses the change, we all do, especially ten minutes before the start. Everyone is aware of the danger of being too relaxed and if the manager thinks we are he will let us know. Some players shout a lot and kick out so they are ready for the first tackle, but I am a player who needs to be relaxed. I'm not playing in a position where I need to be physical from the word go. I've seen videos of rugby players preparing for big confrontations. It looks like character building to me, mental preparation for the first crunching tackle. I just get on with it. We shake hands - that has been the way in all the teams I've played for - and maybe remind each other about a particular point we've discussed. I wish everyone luck on the way out. That's part superstition, part motivation.

For both Wales and Manchester United, the final message is the same. Go out and play, be hard to beat and believe in your own ability. Then, for me, the business starts - on the pitch. My mind is on the match.

THE MATCH

PLAYERS CAN COME TO OLD TRAFFORD AND GO WHITE when they walk out of the tunnel for the start of a game. The stadium can have that effect on you. It has happened to Manchester United players making their home debut, as well as visiting players.

I used to watch Manchester United from Old Trafford's Stretford End as a fan. I was a relatively quiet spectator when I stood behind the goal. Sometimes I joined in with the singing, but mainly I just watched. I know the place and I have got used to it and its atmosphere as a player. But some games, especially games in European competition, still have an impact on me.

It's great when the crowd is behind you during a game. It gives you a real lift, helps you reach a pass and gives you an extra yard of pace. When things are going well and the crowd are letting you know that they appreciate the style of play, I try things that I might otherwise leave for another day. Maybe I will attempt a flick or a turn with the support to encourage me.

I'm lucky. I'm a flair player who looks to entertain and crowds usually get behind this type of player. It also helps that the fans know that I'm a local lad, a homegrown player who has worked his way up through the youth teams at Manchester United. I think that it's easier for a crowd to turn on a player who has joined the club through a transfer.

When we play at Old Trafford, the crowd has expectations. At home we are expected to score three or four goals and win comfortably, like champions. That is fair enough. I can't complain about that. The players have got to try to lift the crowd.

I have played in matches between two entertaining teams which everyone expects to produce a really great game and it just doesn't happen. The crowd can become impatient with what is on show and the atmosphere just dies. If it does, it affects you. Playing for Wales, the

HERE IS AN **ATMOSPHERE.**
ALIVE'

crowd can sometimes be just a fraction of the 50,000 who come to Old Trafford for games. When Wales played San Marino in Italy there were only about 1,000 spectators. It can be hard, but it is up to me to motivate myself in such circumstances. There might be some help from the manager and team-mates, and some noise from the crowd, but it is my responsibility to produce my best and to play well. It is not the fans' job to motivate the players.

When the crowd is against you away from home, I use my head and don't let my heart and feelings affect my game. You must come to terms with it. You can try to work harder to show them how wrong they are about

you, but it never really works. It just encourages them to increase the noise, the shouts and the chanting directed at you. Better to take it as a compliment - if that is possible. If the fans are chanting something vile about me, it isn't exactly a sign that I'm hopeless.

The abuse that fans give players today is worse than it has ever been, but I honestly prefer playing in a noisy stadium, even if the atmosphere is really hostile. Galatasaray in the Champions' League was very intimidating but for me it was the best crowd I have ever experienced. I love it when there is an atmosphere. You're in a game and it is alive. I just love playing with all the noise and excitement in the background. It gets the adrenaline going. Noise, colour, anything, it doesn't

matter. Anything that will raise the tempo of the game and give it an edge.

You can't ever blank out the noise of the fans in the ground. At some grounds on the continent the supporters are nearly 40 yards from the pitch and it is easier to ignore exactly what is being shouted and to concentrate on the match. At other grounds - Barcelona is one, and, at home, there is West Ham - the crowd is right on top of the players. When the home crowd gets behind its own team, it can affect you. It can eat away at your confidence. But wherever I have played there have always been Manchester United fans, the away fans who go to every game, week in, week out. They are always a big encouragement. If things have gone well for me during the first twenty minutes, I can hear the home crowd begin to turn on its own team and players. That lifts me, as well. That sort of bad atmosphere can be good for me and for the whole team.

Some players go into their shells when the atmosphere is intimidating. I'm the opposite. Sometimes I need it. There is nothing worse for me than playing in front of a big crowd that's just sitting and watching. Even booing is better than that. I love playing at Old Trafford, more than anywhere else, but I also love playing at Elland Road against Leeds and against Liverpool at Anfield. What I enjoy most is football. Although the crowd may be hard on me and against me, they share my passion for football. If you don't enjoy the game in front of big crowds, whatever the atmosphere, you will never enjoy it.

When I was seventeen, I was apprehensive about playing at places where the crowd is especially hostile - like Elland Road. But I seemed always to do well against Leeds and that gave me the confidence to enjoy it. The first time Eric Cantona went back to Leeds after being transferred there were death threats. Then there was certainly a slight doubt in the mind about safety. But usually it's not a concern. What's more important is knowing that there are 45,000 people who want you to do badly and when you win, you have beaten them, too.

THE FIRST FIVE MINUTES OF ANY GAME REALLY MATTER. THE FIRST tackle sets the tone. It can have a big bearing on how the game goes. If I can beat the full back, or get a shot in early, it can lift the team and set us up for the rest of the game. My own confidence will rise, too.

The first five minutes of a European tie away from home require a different approach to the domestic game. It is a different mentality, and it requires a different discipline. The games are special, they don't happen every week of the season, and the team is a lot more focused because of them. The game will be tough, the environment could be hostile and unfamiliar, and it's a tougher job all round. Mentally you want to dominate, but you cannot go after your opponents in the first five minutes, flying into tackles as might happen at the start of an FA Cup match or a local domestic derby. The team knows that it must perform as a unit and be controlled.

At first, the approach is quite negative. The forwards have much fewer options at this early stage. When I receive the ball, my main job is simply to hang on to possession in our opponents' half. With the ball at my feet, it is me against the man marking me, but if I lose possession and our opponents have the ball, I'm no longer an individual. I have to become part of the team again. We all have to get behind the ball and keep a shape which will be difficult to break down.

Before a game, every effort is made to plan for all the various formations and tactics we might face. We are usually covered. We always know all about who we are facing before the kick-off - the strength and weaknesses of individuals who have been watched by our scouts - and also that, certainly when we play in Europe, every player lined up against us is likely to be a high quality performer. But sometimes, once the game is underway, the shape of the opposition, exactly which positions individuals are playing, what systems our opponents are planning to play, can surprise us. If the tactics we are playing have to be changed the manager and coach will be screaming instructions and we, as a team, have to be flexible. Sometimes a player is aware of the problem and can take control and make the changes needed to the system, but not always. There are aspects of the game that players who are taking part simply can't see but it will be clear from the manager's view, either from the bench or in the stand. The team has to rely on the manager and the coach. I have a man to mark and I can't be concentrating on what might be the surprise danger that we are facing, or what overall tactics we are up against. Players cannot always see the shape of a game or from where the danger is coming.

Communicating tactical changes can be difficult. There is the noise of the crowd and the pace of the match. As a team, we need to reorganise quickly, especially if we go a goal down in all the confusion. Changes can be made immediately on the pitch. The team is always well briefed and the manager can get instructions across. The manager also has the chance to sort things out in the dressing room at half-time. Whenever it is and whatever the tactical surprise, it is a time for calm thinking. I mustn't panic. If things are going badly, the team has to regroup. We have to make ourselves solid. If our opponents have the ball and they are causing our defence problems so we must become a unit again, a team.

THE GAME ALWAYS HAS A TEMPO. IT BECOMES OBVIOUS VERY quickly. The conditions play a part. If the passing is crisp and the surface is smooth and slick, then the game has a quick tempo. If it is windy and the ground is sticky and tacky, then the game soon slots into a sort of

stop-start rhythm. The play and passing becomes a bit predictable. The tempo picks up when I have a shot at goal or a team-mate wins possession with a strong challenge. The manager can shout at the team and try to lift us, but it usually takes something on the field to happen. It's only natural.

Some players have an aura about them. They inspire me. They are the players who make things happen. The team is always looking to give them the ball. When they have the ball, I always try to make myself available. I know that if I receive a pass it will open up the game for me and the team. These players lead by example. You can see young players playing with them begin to mature and grow from the experience.

The team is lifted by these sorts of players producing some inspiration. When this happens the tempo just quickens automatically. The tempo drops when you score. That's human nature, too. Look at the number of goals that are conceded just after a team has scored. You think, we've scored, and the team stops chasing every ball and tackle. The manager tries to counter it from the touchline - or at half-time - but he is fighting against human nature. Even though it is only a one-goal cushion, it happens. To every team.

When we concede a goal against the run of play, our opponents know it as well as I do. They are not playing well and we have to stick to our own game. When it happens at Old Trafford, we must be patient. I have to have faith in my own ability. Keeping calm when you are 1-0 down is easier said than done. Experience helps me keep the tension under control, but I still feel the anxiety of the situation, and of the crowd. When this happens, the tempo picks up automatically. Things happen faster, which is good because added tempo can produce mistakes in your opponents. But no matter how many games you have played, there's going to be some degree of panic. You must control it.

The mental toughness to cope comes with playing games. Defenders get at you when you are off-form. It is irritating. You can easily begin to think that the match

might be slipping away, but you have to carry on. The defender marking me must not know that I feel like I am struggling. I have to hope that a break comes and that, when it does, I am ready to take advantage of it.

There is added pressure on me, and the front men in the team, because we are expected to be the goal-scorers. It can turn out to be what people call 'one of those days'. The team can have seven or eight chances and not score, or even hit the target. When it is one of those days, all the goals scored on the training ground are no help at all. Sometimes it is as if I could play until midnight and not score.

Then there are also days when anyone who has a chance cannot seem to miss. Everything goes in. That is also 'one of those days'. And both types will always happen in a season.

REFEREES CAN HAVE DAYS WHEN EVERYTHING GOES WRONG. They are human. They make mistakes. They can determine the destiny of a game with one error, but I have to accept that referees are like me; they are human. The game today is quicker and faster than ever before. It's getting harder and harder for referees. Sometimes even television cannot determine what exactly is the correct decision.

Managers are going to criticise referees. The referee's decision affects the manager's future. Managers need results and referees will be attacked when they deny them a win or a draw, or cost them defeat through an error.

I think players should be more sympathetic towards referees. We are all under similar pressures to perform. They have a hard job. There are bound to be mistakes. (And when I am brought down and don't get a penalty I'll probably be the first to say they are all hopeless.) It's hard for me to take to a referee who just walks away when I am talking to him. I prefer referees who want to communicate with players. We are refereed by the same officials three or four times a season each and this helps you to get to know and understand them. I respond to the ones who talk to me or have a joke during the game. It also helps if they are honest enough to admit that they have missed something. For me that brings respect.

Referees in England know that I am not a malicious player. In my position on the wing, I have to make a very bad tackle to receive a yellow card. I don't think about it during league games, only when we play in Europe. On the continent, it can be an unfamiliar referee in charge with his own views of the rule-book. In European games, some players look to dive and get you booked. But in any match there will always be tackles I have to go for.

Playing against a player who is given a yellow card, or who has received cards in previous games, is a big advantage to me, especially in European games. Domestically, if a player receives a yellow card he is one foul away from a red card, and in Europe yellow cards in two games means he misses the next game. If players have taken yellow cards, I take them on at every opportunity. I want to go one on one with them because I know they cannot tackle with complete freedom. I know my opponent has to be careful. I can exploit that.

HALF-TIME CAN OFFER A CHANCE TO REGROUP. SOMETIMES YOU don't want half-time to come, and other times - when the tactics have caught the team by surprise, when the ball is just not running for you - it cannot come soon enough.

Half-time is never a rush. I find the fifteen minutes that we have today is too long. Everything can be done in five minutes. I need a break mentally, but physically I am fine. I could play for sixty or seventy minutes without any sort of break. I just want to hear what the manager has to say and then get back on to the field. The manager sees the whole game and has a clearer picture of things. I may not have thought that I could reach a ball but he will have his view and he may have seen that I would have reached it if I had moved earlier or anticipated things better. He encourages you. Sometimes he shouts. On other occasions he will use the state of games elsewhere to motivate the team. There is no way that the other scores remain secret during the ninety minutes. The crowd and its noise tells the players what is going on around the country. The manager uses it to his advantage. If everyone else is losing, he says that it is a chance to extend a lead or make up ground if we are behind in the league. Sometimes he'll say very little. He'll check on injuries and everyone's fitness and that will be it.

THERE ARE ALWAYS ARGUMENTS DURING A GAME, NO MATTER how well the team gets on. I think it helps build spirit if players argue. It is good for the younger players to shout at the older players. It helps boost their confidence in themselves. I used to argue all the time with my team-mates when I started playing regularly in the first team at Manchester United, even though I was younger. At the end of the game, most people apologise. I might make a joke about it, which means that it is forgotten. It can sometimes continue into the dressing room. But in the end, it is never a problem.

I notice when the opposition are arguing during a game. It is encouraging when they are bickering among themselves. When I see it, it makes me think that I should argue less with my own team-mates. I can see the effect it has and it makes me think before shouting at a team-mate. But I respond to team-mates' shouting. If I am having a bad game and someone has a go at me, then it can help me turn the corner. Other players are different. They need encouraging. They respond better to that than to criticism.

I am not a confrontational type of person. I just want to get on with the game and always have done. But there are times when I think I should have got the ball. When it happens you have to let the player know how you feel. It doesn't happen that often, but it does happen, because I'm passionate about football. I want to win. The crowd can generate passion in players. When the crowd's behind you it makes you more passionate.

Players' personalities can change when they play. Off the pitch, they are calm. You would never imagine that they would argue on the pitch, but players can become completely different people when they are in a game. Whatever the type of player, I would think twice before accusing someone of not trying. If they are not putting every effort into the game, then they will be substituted. You have to be really sure to accuse anyone of not trying 100 per cent. It is a very serious suggestion. You wouldn't make it lightly. I respect all my team-mates.

Sometimes team-mates hit it off straight away. Sometimes it takes a whole season, even two. I have to think what my team-mates' strengths are and play to them and with some players it requires a lot of hard work and thought. I've been lucky. I've played a lot with Denis Irwin, for example, and we understood each other straight away. It was the same with Phil Neville, who sometimes plays at left back. With both it was natural. Teams gel when they play matches. The training ground is not the place where it happens. In training, you are not often in match positions, and it is usually only five- or seven-a-side anyway. You can't develop an understanding in these mini games to the extent that you need for fullscale matches.

THE LAST TWENTY MINUTES OF ANY GAME ARE DEMANDING. Exactly how tough depends on the speed of the game, the tempo. It is both mentally and physically draining. I cannot separate the two feelings of tiredness. Mentally, I become less sharp. As I have gained experience I have got mentally stronger and I now last longer. Physically, it affects me when I have a chance to score. I know what I need to do and still I cannot convert it. Earlier in the game, it might have been straightforward to finish. Some players are fitter than others and cope better. Defenders have an easier time than forwards. Especially when we are chasing a game. Chasing a game is the most demanding type of football there is.

No matter how tired I may be feeling at the time, it's never a relief for me to be substituted. It's always disappointing, the worst thing that can happen for me. I never feel as though I should be substituted. I always believe that I can do something to turn a game. I never want to be off the pitch. I always think that I have something to offer the team.

At games away from Old Trafford, the crowd love it when I'm called off. It doesn't happen very often. If the manager has had a go at me for a mistake and I have shouted back then I suspect it might be coming. Sometimes it's because I have taken a slight knock and I'm injured. But, whatever the reason, the crowd at away games never cares. You have to take it, everything that is being shouted from the stands. Even when you are not happy with coming off, you must not show it.

Sitting on the bench waiting to come on is quite relaxing. There are plenty of jokes among the substitutes and those who don't get on always have something to say about the way the game has gone after the final whistle. Footballers can be cruel like that.

Coming on as a substitute means a complete mental change. I know what the player coming off is feeling as I have felt it myself, but I have to put it out of my mind that he might be steaming with anger. When the manager tells me to warm up I am immediately focused. There will be aspects of the game I have seen from the sidelines and I'll be thinking about how I can exploit weaknesses. It's a lot easier picking up the tempo when we're winning, especially if I am coming back from a spell out injured. I will have done all my stretches and kept warm sitting on the bench, keeping the blood circulating, but it is better to slip back into things without having to chase a game. That can mean a full stretch straight away, even though it's a first game back from a strain or pulled muscle. It takes time to pick up the rhythm of a game no matter how much you've been watching. It is difficult to make any sort of impression in ten minutes, even against opponents who are tired. With half an hour, I know I can make a difference.

WHEN I WAS IN MY TEENS, I WOULD RUN THROUGH IN MY MIND any bad games I had for a long time after the final whistle. It might have been at the end of a run of four or five games when I hadn't managed a goal, or played to my own standards. But you can overcomplicate things. I can go a few games without scoring and then suddenly it all falls into place. That is true for all attackers. It's also true for goalkeepers. Things suddenly click for them. At both ends of the field, results hinge on the performances of keepers and strikers.

I used to think a lot more about my form in games. I'd ask the manager how he felt I was playing. I would worry that players were not giving me the ball because they had lost confidence in me. I've changed with experience. I know I can't become a bad player just like that. I know I just have to work a bit harder during the game.

Footballers live in a closed world. The teasing and banter when you are off your game can be worse than when you're playing well. Footballers can be evil like that. The teasing reminds me that I am a good player. They wouldn't be on my back otherwise. You cannot play at the level that I play and not be confident about your own ability. You have to believe in yourself all the time, when you play badly and score twice, or when you have a great game and don't get on the score sheet. You've got to keep faith. During a match, the chances will come, and you have got to be mentally ready for them.

AFTERWARDS

I REMEMBER MOST OF WHAT HAS HAPPENED IN A GAME. Afterwards, in the dressing room, I talk to my team-mates about what took place, the controversial moments. They can stay in my head for a long time after the final whistle. At night after a game, I sometimes lie there thinking about a chance that I missed, an easy opportunity I should have taken. Some games, when things have gone wrong, can seem longer than others when you think back over the ninety minutes.

Straight after the match in the dressing room, there's no detailed analysis as a team of how things have gone. It's heat of the moment stuff. The manager either praises us or he gives us a dressing down for the way we have played. I think it's good to get things like that off your chest. They should be discussed straight away. If you play Saturday and then some of the team have the Sunday off, the thought has passed by Monday. It has gone and it won't be discussed before we play again. If we don't discuss our mistakes, then we are not going to improve.

We can all get angry after a game. The manager can have a go at me straight away in the dressing room. He can single out me - or a team-mate - and criticise the way I've played, even when I might feel I've done well. It's no bad thing to experience. It can be character building. I will stick up for myself if I think he is wrong. Some players might think it's easier just to agree if the manager has a go at them a couple of weeks in a row. I am too committed to the team and to doing well to accept criticism if it is not fair or justified. I'm passionate about football and my own performance, so I am going to argue my point of view even in the face of disagreement. We are all in it together, but that doesn't mean we can't disagree. It is healthy that we sometimes do.

'I RARELY TAKE A DAY OFF'

For a home game, we largely go our separate ways afterwards. I don't hang around. I usually go home. Away games are different. We are together for the journey so we talk about the game at greater length as we travel back to Manchester. For big European games I sometimes get back home only in the small hours. But after a big game, I can't sleep anyway so I may as well be travelling. I want to be home, to relax. For a European tie, we sometimes stay overnight, but I would always really rather travel back home straight away after the match is over.

Winding down after a big game is difficult. If it's an evening kick-off, I may not be able to fall sleep before two o'clock in the morning. After the game, my brain is still alive with the match. Even on a boring coach journey. If the game has been on television and I am home in time, I might watch a rerun at around midnight, depending on how the game has gone. The adrenaline is still running through the veins and I have probably had a sleep in the afternoon so I'm still wide awake. I feel more tired two days after an evening game than the morning after. The sleep on the second night is a deeper sleep. I feel very tired after an afternoon game as soon as the adrenaline wears off. By ten in the evening I begin to feel the effect of my efforts. I'm ready to sleep. There isn't the same time after an evening game for me to unwind, so I don't relax until the small hours at the earliest.

If we have drawn, I feel like we have lost . The expectations are so high for Manchester United it means that a draw is a disappointment. I want to win games and when I draw I haven't achieved my aim. Straight after the game I may not feel that way, or as strongly about it. The game and result might drift out of my thoughts, but I will end up feeling very disappointed later when I think over the game at home on my own.

I don't get angry. I get upset and frustrated. I mull over the game, and think about moments when I might have tried something different, something that might have swung things our way. There's always some aspect of play, some moment during the ninety minutes when, looking back, I think I could have attempted something different or performed better. Something that might have made the difference between winning handsomely and drawing, or getting nothing out of the game.

When I was younger, I would sulk if I lost. I was so hungry to win. I am still a bad loser. I want to win everything. I get frustrated with myself when things are not going well. After a bad result I can snap at people around me. People who know me are well aware of this. I give people a look. I am renowned for it. It is just the way I am. I can't change it. I think there is a danger that I might lose my competitive edge if defeat didn't hurt as much as it still does.

I have mellowed and matured a little with time and experience. I still get upset about bad results, but I'm able to put them behind me much more quickly. I try to look forward, look ahead to the next game, instead of thinking about a setback for a day or two.

As a team, we always want to win the league. Each year, it is important to win your own top trophy. It's not something you can put to one side. Tomorrow may never come. I want to win things every year, starting with the league. Winning the league means you are the best team in the country. That is a great feeling. All the players certainly enjoy it. And the fans always want us to win the league.

I might now accept not winning the league if the club won the European Champions' Cup, but that has not always been the case. When I first made it into the first team, winning the league was an obsession. The desire to do well in Europe now is not as strong as the desire to win the league was when I began to play in the first team in 1990. Then, it was simply, 'Let's win the league.' We won the FA Cup in 1990, which was fine, but afterwards it was, 'Great, now let's win the league.' It didn't change much when we won the European Cup Winners' Cup the following season, which was thrilling, but then again it was, 'Fine, now let's win the league.'

Individual awards have never been that important to me. The players all take them seriously, but I consider winning something for myself as a bonus. Nobody thinks about it at the beginning of the season. It only enters your mind after you have been nominated. Playing with Eric Cantona is the only experience I have had when one individual has done so much for a team. Eric was scoring goals. He was the main man, everybody knew that. But no matter what was being said about Eric Cantona, and how many personal awards he eventually won, he knew he couldn't do anything without the rest of the team and we all knew that as well.

After a hard game, I stretch all my leg muscles - hamstrings, thighs, calves - to keep me physically in shape. This is to avoid injury in the future. It will help keep me supple. Being supple means I'm less likely to pull a muscle the next time I play. I stretch more than most players, but others stretch particular problem areas more vigorously - Peter Schmeichel and Gary Pallister stretch their backs, for example - areas they will also have worked on before the game.

For Wales, I warm down. That means I go on to the pitch with the rest of the team to stretch after the match. I get help from the physio and do a bit of stretching myself, and I also do some jogging across the pitch. There is no similar warm-down at Manchester United. Some physios believe in it, some don't. At Manchester United, the routine is to come in the day after the match and do some jogging to get all the 'rubbish' out of the legs. I rarely take a day off. It's important to come in the day after a game and have a massage or a hot bath.

I can be stiff for a couple of days after a difficult game. But once I have stretched and warmed up I can train comfortably. Stiffness is a different problem to a pulled muscle. A pull or strain limits what I can do on the training ground. The stiffness does not restrict me and it eventually goes during the morning.

If I have been injured in the game and we are travelling back to Manchester, I may have to keep mobile during some of the journey. It isn't good to be sitting down for a long period if I have, say, strained my hamstring. I have to walk up and down the coach or plane every now and then to stop the muscle tightening up any more until I can receive the full attention and treatment of the physio.

I KNOW SOME PLAYERS WHO ENCOURAGE THEIR FRIENDS TO video Match of the Day if they have scored a hat trick. I might do that too - if I ever manage to score a hat trick. If I have had a really bad game, I don't see the point of watching it again on television straight away that evening, even if I cannot sleep. Although I have plenty

of confidence in my ability to perform next time, my self-belief can only be undermined if I watch myself having a nightmare game. That evening, what can I do about it? It is possible to overanalyse and overcomplicate things by watching yourself too much.

The day after a game, the manager might sit me down and have a word with me about an aspect of my play the day before, or on Monday about something that happened on Saturday. The manager has a different view of games. Watching myself on video with the manager so he can make his points can help me to see his different perspective of things, his view from the bench or the stands. If I have been criticised by the manager after the game, I might have disagreed, but by watching a video of the game with him I can clearly see the thought behind the point he made immediately in the dressing room and why he made it then. I will always listen to advice like this, well-explained advice. If I have made a mistake I want to correct it. If I listen to criticisms that help then that is good. If the comments are

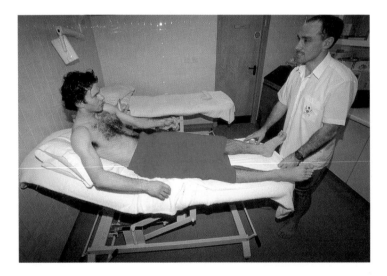

no help, at least I have listened. If I don't agree I will go with my instincts and I always stick to my way if I don't think the person is right. But I always want to have one-to-one chats with the coaches. I ask them, or they pull me aside for a talk. They have my best interests and the team's best interests at heart. I always listen to advice.

I watch more football on television now than I have ever done. This is partly because today more is screened than ever before, but it also reflects a greater dedication that comes with age. Some players seek responsibility immediately for the way the team is going to play. They have always looked for greater insight into football from watch-

ing games on television. They study every match they play in and other games as well.

I certainly don't think I could do without watching football on television altogether. But it's more a case of watching because I'm at home relaxing before a game of my own and a match happens to be on. I wouldn't necessarily stay in just to watch a game. Only if I am in anyway. But I am now older, more mature, and more aware of the benefits of watching games.

I now see the game as being much more complex than I used to. From watching myself playing and from watching other teams' games, I have learnt more about playing in other positions, about the dangers of giving the ball away at critical times, and about the extra responsibilities that there are in different areas of the field for my team-mates and for me when I find myself filling their positions.

I analyse individuals. I look at a player I admire and try to assess what he is good at and where his weaknesses are. I think of ways that I can adapt my game to beat him when I next find myself opposing him. But I don't just see things in isolation any more, only from my own point of view. If you are a player like Andy Cole, who is an out and out striker, you might be able to focus on just your markers, the defenders who will be facing you through the season. But I am not isolated on the wing any more, only worrying about the full backs that I will be facing. I may also be asked to play in midfield and I have to be prepared to do more for the team. I must be prepared to do my best wherever I find myself.

INTERNATIONAL FOOTBALL ALSO OFFERS ME THE CHANCE TO improve my game by learning from players, both team-mates and opponents, from a wide range of backgrounds. That is a positive thing. A negative aspect of international football is that, because of FIFA rules, it can mean up to a ten-day break from domestic matches, which can disrupt the rhythm of Manchester United. I think that club sides could do without these breaks during the season. It's true that a break can be good for a side if things are not going well - it's good for players who have been playing badly together in the league to go away for a week and join their respective national squads and to train with other players - but generally it disrupts the season which then becomes broken up.

If I don't have a game for Wales and there are other international matches, then I train with the reserves. That makes for a quiet week. My Manchester United team-mates travel to play in games for their own national teams: England, Norway, Ireland, Holland and Denmark. I think that club sides could certainly do without the

week-long break just for friendly games. They are not World Cup or European Championship qualifiers and they are not the same as the real thing, when qualifying points for a major championship are at stake. Players prepare for friendlies differently. A friendly should demand the same preparation as any match for your country. After all, it is an international. But it never works like that. There's not the same coverage in the media, and the fans are not as enthusiastic. It's human nature that preparation for such games is not as concentrated, no matter how hard the players focus. There isn't the same buzz.

For Wales, we need a lot of luck and for all our best players to be available if we are going to do well. We don't have the same numbers of players to draw on that England has. We need things to go right for us to do well and if they do we really can achieve something. Scotland, Ireland and Northern Ireland are all in the same position as Wales, and they have achieved success. We can beat the teams we need to beat to qualify for

World Cups and European Championships. I know that because we have come so close in the past.

I HAVE KNOWN SOME OF MY MANCHESTER UNITED TEAM-MATES for a long time now, on the field and off it. Some are good friends. I've grown up with the younger members of the team. We've been together for years. But it's not just about time. It is about shared experiences. That is why I can be close to the older players as well. I've been in the team with Gary Pallister for years now. We have been through different experiences and shared highs and lows as players. The highs and lows, success and failure - they bring you closer together.

With retirements and players being transferred, you can lose the closeness that builds up over time and from playing together season after season. I will chat with players who have left the club when I see them after a game, but some part of the old relationship has gone through their leaving the club. There's no longer any banter. Down the line, I might see an old team-mate who was transferred a couple of years back. I'll say hello, but it's not the same. Having played football for representative sides since I was a teenager, I know a lot of the players who are now playing Premier League foot-ball. But even though I haven't known my team-mates for anything like the same length of time, I'm closer to them. I might chat for ten minutes to a player I've grown up with and who plays for another club, but that's it.

I signed a long-term contract with Manchester United. I don't want to go anywhere else. Knowing that I'm contracted to be with the club until I'm twenty-nine makes me feel more valued by them. I understand that the Bosman court ruling has meant that clubs have an incentive to keep their players on longer contracts so they don't lose them for a free transfer when the contracts run out, but, even so, I still feel that the club is more committed to me by offering me a long-term deal. I signed the longest contract I've ever had and that makes me feel good about the future.

LIFE

My life has never been as crazy as the lives of people who appear in soap operas on television, or pop stars and film celebrities. There are many more positives than negatives to my life. I might be in the general spotlight once a year for something I've done, or something that has happened to me, but most of the time I can go about my life. I can go into Manchester city centre if I want, no problem. Or I can walk the dogs in the area around where I live. Manchester is a great city. The people who live in and around Manchester may notice me in the town or out in the street. They may point me out to their friends or whoever they are with, but, generally speaking, they don't bother me. They leave me to myself and respect my privacy.

For me, Manchester is a friendly place. I can go to the local pub or a local restaurant. I've been going to the same places to meet friends for years. These are places where I've grown up. That helps. I've also learnt from experience. I know there are some places that I cannot visit; some things that I can do and some things that I can't.

After training, I always try to sign autographs for the people who come to the Cliff, where we train, and wait for the players to leave. It comes naturally to me now. If I'm out shopping or in a restaurant having a meal and somebody comes up and asks me for an autograph I just give it to them. Some people say to me that it must feel strange signing autographs or having my picture taken by people I've never met before but I don't think of it as strange. Not any more. I know that I don't have a normal life, but for me there is nothing in it that isn't normal. Now it's much easier for me. When I was still in my teens it was harder, but I learnt quickly. Today, I try very hard not to become withdrawn. I have the same friends that I've always had and I try to do normal things with them, things that anyone my age would want to do.

I could sign 999 autographs and, after that, if I didn't sign one more it could be held against me. It is a fine line. If I am a role model for people it also means that if I do one thing that damages my reputation in their eyes then it could be held against me for ever. The

'I DON'T HAVE A NORMAL LI BUT THERE

profession I am in is getting more and more high profile. The money I earn seems to be a fair deal for the sacrifices I might have to make. I don't expect anyone to do me any favours. It doesn't really matter how many autographs I am expected to sign, it's fair that I am asked. It doesn't bother me how many cameras are on me when I'm training or playing in a game. I accept that.

I always have to remember the amount of energy I need to play professional football. That is both physical and mental energy. I need to relax away from the pressure so that I am ready for the demands of the game. I need to rest properly.

I have become more disciplined in this respect as I have grown older. You learn. I appreciate the value of rest more now. When I was younger the manager would tell me to go home and put my feet up and rest my legs, even just for a couple of hours. When you're younger you have more energy, but you appreciate the value of such advice with time. Now, I feel tired physically after training and I know that I have to rest. When I was seventeen I used to go out every afternoon once we had finished training. I got by without too much trouble, but now I like to come home and just relax, two or three times a week after training has finished.

I turn down more commercial work than I could possibly find the time to do. The amount I have to say no to is unbelievable. Football is my main business. It is what I do, and I cannot do anything that might interfere with that so the answer to offers of work off the field often has to be no. I cannot take on a project that will

OTHING IN IT THAT ISN'T NORMAL'

affect my football. In the second half of the season the games come thick and fast so I take on very few commitments outside playing. I don't want to be doing any commercial work that might distract me from my game, or affect my performance.

I have tried to take on bigger projects that require less time overall. It's better than committing myself to lots of small projects every week. I have always been advised, by Harry Swales my manager, that it's better to take on five or six major commercial projects a year with big companies that are not going to mess me around, than to get tied up in lots of time-consuming things.

I have no problem with turning on the television and seeing myself on the screen promoting a product, or opening a magazine and seeing my face in an advert, or looking up and seeing myself on a billboard. It's not something that has happened overnight. It's like my progress in football. Things have developed gradually and I have got used to it slowly, over time. It comes with the job. As I have got more experienced I have taken on more and more commercial work and I have become better equipped to handle different requests.

I'd rather have my photograph taken for an advertisement than open a supermarket or a shop. Once I have committed to it, it's just a couple of hours in an afternoon. If I have to have my photograph taken, I try to be as professional as possible. That way it is over quickly. I just get on with it. The more photo shoots I do the easier they become. I have even come to enjoy them. And if I don't think I will enjoy it, I won't agree to it. I wouldn't agree to photo shoots if I felt uncomfortable doing them. No one wants to do something they hate. Paul Scholes doesn't like this side of being a professional footballer for Manchester United. But for me, it is not tiring mentally. It can actually be quite relaxing, as long as the photographer doesn't expect me to pull funny faces or stand on my head. It is also a break from the routine. I am going to a studio for the afternoon instead of sitting at home. I have no problem with it.

When you are younger you might agree to do things which you later regret having done. With all commercial projects, as long as I am in control, I am happy. Football is a short career. Many of the offers I receive to do promotional work are so good I would be stupid to turn them down. I just have to make sure that I don't take on anything that affects my game. And an afternoon of photographs won't.

IF SOMETHING HAS HAPPENED TO ME AT THE CLUB, OR IN MY personal life, and I am out doing an appearance or a photo shoot, then I keep it inside. I hide any stress I'm under. That's one of my faults. I don't talk about myself as much as I should. I bottle things up for about a week, then it comes out and I explode. After that, I'm all right. People who know me well, and have known me for a long time, can spot when I'm under pressure. They worry - my family and friends, that is - and I tell them that I'm fine, really, and that they shouldn't worry.

The difference for me is that it's not just my friends and family who know when I have a problem. I face the same problems as everybody else and have to cope, but with me everyone knows what's going on in my life. Everyone knows about me and that's one of the things about my life that I find very difficult to cope with. It goes with the job. I understand that. But I don't think it is always fair. It is not fair when there are cameramen from the newspapers camped outside my house. But it doesn't bother me any more. It used to, but I don't let it get to me now. I used to worry what other people (who read the papers) would think about me. But now I don't care. I am single-minded about everything. I only worry about what the people I care about think.

Training is a break from all the attention. Playing the game is a relief from all the pressure off the field of being a Manchester United footballer. The pitch is away from all the hassles. I feel safe when I'm on the pitch. On the pitch, I'm doing what I do best and what I love doing and no one can take that away from me. It's where I feel comfortable.

OUTSIDE FOOTBALL, I EXPECT SOME PRIVACY AND TO HAVE MY private life respected. It bothers me when it's not. That is just the way that Britain is. It's all gossip. People seem to need to know what the famous people are up to. People love reading the newspapers and watching television to find out what the stars are doing. You'll hear someone say they are not interested, but you'll still catch them reading the front page of the paper.

My friends are like everyone else. They read the papers. I always say to them, I don't know why you bother because half the stories in the paper aren't true. In some of them, the main thread of the story might

have some truth to it, but I know from my own experience that some of the quotes in it will have been made up. I don't bother with stories in the paper about me. I look at the pictures in the newspapers. But I don't really read the stories.

I do speak to my friends about stories in the paper about footballers at other clubs. I know they are not 100 per cent true, but I have an interest in the game, and I share that with my friends, which means we talk about transfer news. Of course, if you're a footballer you're interested in other footballers. The manager always says we shouldn't read the papers. He reckons we all know the story, so what's the point. He's right. When I read what's written I don't take it seriously.

Being in the public eye is a lot harder for footballers than it is for soap stars. We can be seen at places where people might be doing things that could affect our match performance. A footballer might be photographed leaving a pub. And even if he hasn't been drinking, newspaper readers might think that, if he has a bad game, it's because he went out to the pub. Pop stars aren't judged like that because they don't need what I need to perform. They may work hard, but they don't need to rest to the same extent as footballers do. If people go to see a pop concert and it's a poor performance, they don't criticise the singer for not having rested enough before the start. Footballers have to be seen to be living boring lives.

MY PERFECT DAY, IF I WASN'T TRAINING, WOULD START WITH A lie-in. I don't get many. It's rare that I'm not up at a reasonable time. Then I'd have breakfast and afterwards go for a game of golf with some friends. After eighteen holes, I'd relax and have something to eat. A day without pressure.

When I was at school I wanted to get out of the house all the time, every day of the week, but now when there is pressure in my life all I want to do is stay in. I want to be where I'm most comfortable, and that's my home.

I know I won't be bothered there. People won't be looking at me, and I'll be with people with whom I'm comfortable and who are comfortable with me. I'll be totally relaxed.

If I become bored watching television, or just sitting in at home during an afternoon, I can go out and visit a friend. Sometimes I play golf, although at times the manager bans us from playing so that we rest. I use common sense about what I should and should not do during the season outside playing football. On holiday I'm also sensible. I don't try horse-riding. I can water-ski but I don't very much. I'm not allowed to go skiing. I'd probably be all right, but there's always the chance of an accident. And I don't want to injure myself and have to miss games. It's a small sacrifice and one I'm happy to make because the most important thing to me is that I'm fit to play at the start of the season after a break away from it all.

I have always liked shopping. It's not as if I go into every shop in town. I drive into the city centre and go to one or two shops that I know. I know what I want. I hate window shopping. I hate the sort of shopping where you have to walk around looking at shop after shop. I do all my Christmas shopping on Christmas Eve. But I've always liked nice clothes. It's also a distraction, something to do. I shop because I like clothes and I like buying the clothes, it's a bit of both. Something to do that I enjoy.

At the end of the season I'm sick of football. It's not that I don't like it any more. It's just that I need a break. I can't wait for the rest. It's not physical, it's mental. I need to go away and get some sun. I need to relax. But after three or four weeks, I begin to feel bored. I begin to want to be back, training. I've always wanted to practise. No one's ever told me I need to work harder. I can spend three weeks just lying on the beach in the sun. That's no problem at all. But after a while I want to get back to playing football, to get back to training. I do get sick of the game, certainly, but my appetite always returns for the challenges of a new season.

RESULTS

I AM ALWAYS CONFIDENT OF SUCCESS. I HAVE BEEN IN A TEAM that's managed to win plenty of trophies - four championships, two FA Cups and a League Cup. Every year I expect that we will end up winning something. But then again I don't walk around for the whole year telling everyone I meet that we are going to win the league. There is always the thought at the back of my mind that we might end up with nothing.

Losing the league and giving up the title of champions doesn't hit you straight away. At the end of the season, I always just feel relief. Whatever the outcome, it will have been a long, hard ten months and I will not have had a break. I look forward to going away somewhere warm just to relax. The hurt of losing the league - in 1997/8 to Arsenal, in 1994/5 to Blackburn, and to Leeds before then - comes later. It is an empty feeling.

Losing the Cup Final hits you on the day. There's no delay. Like not qualifying for the World Cup with Wales when we had a great chance to make it to America in 1994. That hit me immediately. Not making it to the final of the FA Cup also hits you on the day of the game at Wembley, whoever is playing. All my team-mates know that the FA Cup is a huge competition, with the final the biggest game of the season. It is a great game to play in and a great occasion. I always watch it, just out of interest, like any football supporter. As I watch, I think, I want to be there. Seeing two other teams playing in the Cup Final on television, I remember how much I enjoyed playing in past finals myself.

Right at the end of the season in 1992, after we had lost the league to Leeds, it was a case of asking ourselves, will we ever win the league? The club hadn't won the championship for over twenty years at that

'IN EVERY **SEASON** THERE WILL BE GAMES THAT GIVE **REAL SATISFACTION**'

time. After Arsenal - and Blackburn - there was some comfort in the thought that I had at least helped the club to come second. Then it doesn't seem like all the hard work has been a total waste of time and effort. It's a great achievement to finish second in the league. But eventually, during the summer, that feeling is replaced by one of disappointment. Then I begin simply to think that I worked hard all year to win the league and in the end we didn't.

Arsenal made up ground on us in the last three months of the 1997/8 season. We had the points, they had games in hand. Although they ultimately won it, I'd still always take the pressure of being in front with the points already earned. When you play for Manchester United, there is always pressure, with people saying we are going to win the league again, and with everyone wanting to beat us. I'd rather cope with that pressure while the club is top of the league, than be in second place and chasing the leaders, whoever they might be.

Arsenal were already champions with two games to go before the end of the season. We played at home against Leeds on May Bank Holiday Monday, the day after Arsenal picked up the last three points they needed, at Highbury against Everton on the first Sunday of the month. Our game was weird. It was Leeds at Old Trafford, one of the big games of the year, and I wanted to win for the supporters as it was the last home game of the season. In the end we won comfortably, 3-0. But it was more relaxed than the fixture usually is. I scored very early on which made it even more laid-back.

The season's final game was away at Barnsley. It was also strange. They were already relegated and we were guaranteed second place, whatever the result. But they still wanted to win in front of their own fans, and we had lots of younger players in the side who wanted to do well to impress the manager. We won 2-0. My Manchester United team-mates who are in the England squad had been given the game off to rest for the World Cup in France. It felt funny without so many of the established players. A strange end to the season.

During the year, the team's most disappointing spell for me was when we were beaten by Leicester at home at the end of January and then drew with Bolton, also at Old Trafford. We underperformed in front of our own fans and that is always bad. The highlights of the year as a team were against Juventus at home in the European Champions' League when we won 3-2, and in the FA Cup third round against Chelsea at Stamford Bridge when we were 5-0 up before finally winning 5-3. The game at home against Juventus was a huge game for Manchester United. And a professional footballer will always want to prove himself against the very best in Europe. Against Chelsea, we were just flying.

In every season there will be games like Juventus and Chelsea that give real satisfaction. They are what really makes being a professional footballer, what you train hard for, what you hope for when putting in all the work and preparation.

MY FAMILY AND FRIENDS WILL NOT EVEN MENTION IT WHEN things on the field are not going as well as they have done in the recent past. My old friends from home and school still come round to see me whatever the results have been. We all go out, as usual. We just talk about different things, not football. It is quite odd. Maybe for them it's a bit of a taboo subject. No one wants to bring up bad news in front of the person it involves. I don't know - I think they might perhaps be a bit wary. They might be wondering how I will react if they mention the game when I have played poorly or been substituted. They may decide that it's better not to talk about it with me.

Being substituted at Highbury was a big personal disappointment of Arsenal's championship season. We eventually lost the game 3-2 to a late goal, having got back from 2-0 down to 2-2. I know myself that I didn't play well and was very down about it. But it's not the same as when you finally accept that the team hasn't won the league. I get angry when I've had a bad game, especially if I've been substituted. But at least there's always another game to look forward to soon, usually in a matter of days. After the defeat at Arsenal on Sunday, there was the game against Wimbledon a fortnight later, which we won 5-2. You want to play again soon and put things right and in this case I had the chance. You can't do that when the season is over and the league is lost.

The end to the '98 season was spoiled for me when I got injured against Derby in February. That was a major disappointment. I had felt that I was playing really well and up to that point I had been injury-free nearly all season. Then my hamstring went.

I was injured and out of the side only for about five weeks, but it was at a crucial time, with league matches and the quarter finals of the Champions' League against Monaco, which I missed. It meant that when it was really important to me I was not able to do what I love: playing football. It was frustrating. I didn't know exactly when I would be back from injury. If you know you'll be back in a couple of games it is easier to cope with, but any more games than that and it becomes very hard.

I came back for a big game against Blackburn in April which went very well. I had a long sprint in the first five minutes which really tested the hamstring. But it made it all the more disappointing that I then had to go off in the Liverpool game four days later with a recurrence of the injury. That was after only thirty-five minutes. Everything had been fine against Blackburn and then against Liverpool I felt the leg again. I had to ask to be substituted.

Even though I missed games at the most important stage of the season, I still felt, at the end of it, after Arsenal had won the double, that I had been through the same pressure as the rest of the players had. It's a team game, and everyone feels the same about losing. There is disappointment throughout the club, but I think that the players feel it more than any other group.

I'm not a great loser, but I don't think that's necessarily a bad thing. I don't think you should ever get used to losing. The manager certainly makes sure that that will never happen. I admire the way he can say at the end of the season that Arsenal deserved to win the league ahead of us, that they were the best team, that any team that could put together the run that they did in the last third of the season deserve to be champions. I can't say it, myself. Maybe the ability to say something along those lines comes with age. I suppose I am more capable now than I was when I was younger of saying when we lose that we deserved to get beaten. But I suspect I will be saying it through gritted teeth for some time yet.

Personal recognition is some compensation for the team's disappointment. A Player of the Year award can soften the blow of a losing season. It tells me that I did my best and that no one really believes I could have done any more than I did. You may not have won anything, but you personally have had a good season and the fans, who vote for their player of the year, have a chance to show their appreciation.

Milestones are the same. I scored the fiftieth goal of my career in the dead game against Leeds at the end of the season at Old Trafford. I didn't know it was the fiftieth until somebody told me afterwards - I've never kept track of how many times I've played or the goals I've scored - but it was nice, either way.

I wore the captain's armband for the first time, against Barnsley. I was the most experienced member of the team the manager put out that day. It made me proud to lead them. I decided just to enjoy the day as I don't expect the honour to come round again soon. The only difficulty I had with the responsibility was that the armband kept slipping off. I'll be working on the weights.

WHEN THE NEW SEASON BEGINS I CARRY OVER NO GRUDGES against any particular team. I don't look at the fixture list to see when we are playing Arsenal. The Premier League is not about settling old scores from the previous year. It is not about beating Arsenal on its own. It is about finishing ahead of everybody on the last day of the season. I don't think about the previous year's games when the new season has started. The only time I look at the fixture list is near the end of the season. It's only then that it matters, when it's worth seeing which of the title contenders has the easiest of run-ins. Then you think about hard games ahead, but not before. But every game is like a Cup Final for Manchester United. I know it sounds corny, but it is true. You just get used to it.

I find it exciting when the manager buys players for the new season over the summer - and throughout the year. Ultimately, I am a United fan as well as a player. I simply want the best for Manchester United. I want the best players to come to the club and to play for the benefit of the club. You wouldn't even think I was a player when I'm talking to my friends about the transfer market. I'm always the one saying how I'd love the club to buy so and so. I want the best for the club. Transfer buys of quality footballers are for the good of United. I never consider the manager might be buying someone to replace me. Even if the manager bought a left-winger I wouldn't worry. I have confidence in my ability.

At the start of the new season, after a year of winning nothing, I can sense that the team wants to do well. Nobody has to say anything to anyone. I can just feel that the players want to win something badly. When we've won nothing I feel there is a debt to the fans from the previous season. That does mean more pressure to do well, but I am playing for Manchester United and I accept that. If you didn't then you wouldn't be playing for the club.

Sometimes it is good to lose, to make sure that the appetite is still there. Losing re-establishes the fear of defeat that motivates me to win. The team also comes closer together when it has setbacks and disappointments. Shared experiences bring players together and if we've had a season without success at the end of it, you become closer because of it. That has been the case with Gary Pallister. We've been through a lot together, having

played together for so long. Now, after finishing second behind Arsenal, it is also the case with Paul Scholes, and the other younger players. The 1998 season was the first time that the players younger than me had played a full part with the first team and not ended up with a trophy, so as a team we are now stronger.

There may be greater expectations on me, personally, from now on. When I was out injured during 1998, fans in Manchester would say that the team missed me, and that the club could do with me back fit and playing. Although that means pressure, it is a positive pressure. It motivates me. I take it as a compliment. It is not a burden. It works as an inspiration. When Eric Cantona was suspended for kicking a fan, he was a different class on his return. He knew the team had missed him. When he came back he knew that he needed to perform to his very best.

When training starts for a new season, every new season, I'll be back, and I'll want to finish first. In everything. I always do.

Photograph by Ryan's mum

John Peters on photographing
Ryan Giggs

I STARTED IN PHOTOGRAPHY taking publicity pictures for Granada Television studios and for theatres like the Royal Exchange, in Manchester where I have always lived. I became involved in photographing sport only through a friend of mine. Funnily enough, he worked on the Manchester City match day programme.

As you can imagine, working with footballers is very different to dealing with actors. In television and the theatre, there can be the advantage of artificial lighting. Subjects from the arts and entertainment are also more used to being personally scrutinised at close quarters. Publicity photographs are part of their trade. That is understood.

Footballers are doing me a favour by letting me use them as subjects. It's not really part of their job and they don't have to do it if they don't want to. I remember photographing Eric Cantona for his return to football after serving a ban for attacking a fan. He allowed me only three shots. 'If there is not a good picture from those then you are not a good photographer,' was his explanation. He had his eyes closed for one of them! But one was good enough for the cover of a magazine.

Ryan is much less demanding and a lot more helpful. He is also a natural. He started having his photograph taken when he was seventeen and by the time I started working with him two years later he was very professional, a real star.

He prefers serious shots of himself, the moody look which I enjoy capturing on film and have reproduced effectively both in colour, as here, and in black and white. It can sometimes be hard to get a smile out of him. If I do manage to, I reckon it's because I've worked with him over a long period of time. He now relaxes completely when I'm photographing him. Over the years, we have built up a good working relationship and plenty of trust.

Some of the best pictures of Ryan I took for this book were when he was just a little off-guard. I might take shots of him before we formally start a session, or afterwards, when he is relaxing because he has finished and thinks it's all over. This partly explains why he photographs so well on the pitch. He is concentrating on playing and is off-guard as far as the camera is concerned. He is doing his job and I am doing mine.

I wanted the cover shot to reflect everything about Ryan Giggs the footballer. It shows him after a match at the end of the working day, the job done, last to leave, dressed to go home. It represents the culmination of all his efforts during the week, and is taken at the heart of Old Trafford, the players' dressing room.

The other photographs in the book I hope illustrate the rest of Ryan's life, his preparation and devotion to his job as a professional footballer for Manchester United, and the gentle, quiet side of him that is considerate towards people who are less fortunate than himself, and for whom he always has time.